I0429851

Emancipating Bantu Africans From Poverty

George Malonje Mwanza

Copyright © 2014 George Malonje Mwanza

All rights reserved.

ISBN-10: 1501068547
ISBN-13: 978-1501068546

DEDICATION

This book is dedicated to hundreds of millions of dispossessed and impoverished Bantu Africans.

CONTENTS

ACKNOWLEDGMENTS

For all my passion in research and writing, I would not be published without the assistance, generosity, and insights of other people and writers. Indeed, mine is eternal gratitude to many people whose ideas, technical assistance, and support have made this book a reality. Particularly, I am deeply indebted to Mr Patrick S. Filter, my philosophy lecturer, who even after I had left college went on to nurture my writing interest with books on writing and physically tutored me to write honestly and with style. Chassa Secondary School (Sinda) with its many helpful teachers and staff deserve a special mention too. They not only lent me a number of books I used in my research for this book but also gave me some technical assistance with computers. Finally, for me to end up really published, having been writing for about 20 years now, I owe it to Dr Teddy Andrew Mulenga MD M Media. He encouraged me to strive to get my works published, offered to look at this work, recommended it for publication, had it edited, and prepared it for publication.

EPIGRAM

Africa is our own motherland,

Let us all her people own our lands.

Owning our lands and property is our cry,

Dignity and prosperity for us all.

#Letsown.

PROLOGUE

The Parable

Of

Bantu Orphans

The reason I speak to them in parables is that they look without seeing and listen without hearing or understanding.

—Jesus Christ, Mathew 13: 13-14.

I came upon the parable of Bantu Orphans, not from the Holy Scriptures nor the Dead Sea Scrolls, but among the many heart-rending, living tales of perpetual want and deprivation in Africa,

especially Bantu Africa—East, Central, and Southern Africa—
Mzansi.

There it is learnt that not so long ago there lived an
enormously rich couple, Bantu and Zanji, and their four
adolescent children—Nkhosi, Apao, Uhuru, and Nzika. Bantu
and his family owned all the gold, diamonds, emeralds, copper,
silver, domestic and wild animals, and the vast lands of Mzansi
that contained them.

Using this tremendous wealth, Bantu built himself and his
family a treasure-villa with a million rooms. These rooms, like
the treasure-villa itself, which people simply called Bantu
House, were amazing. Each room was as big as a football pitch
and, like the entire Bantu House, constructed out of pure golden
bricks and molten copper as mortar. And then all their many
doors were made of ivory; windows, emerald and diamond
glass; and roofs, pure silver. While such extravagance alone
astounded many observers, the ingenuity of building this
treasure-villa across so many mighty rivers, the Congo, the
Zambezi, the Luangwa and the Limpopo; the sophistication of
channelling these mighty rivers' waters into all the one million
rooms, making them all self-contained; and the audacity of
turning the mammoth water bodies of lake Victoria, lake
Tanganyika, lake Malawi, and lake Cabora Bassa into luxurious,
in-house swimming pools—all mystified those who visited and
entered Bantu House.

Bantu House, nevertheless, was too vast for Bantu, his wife,
and their four children to live in alone. So in another surprising
act, Bantu let thousands of his unoccupied, golden, self-
contained rooms teem with all sorts of Mzansi creatures that
would make Noah's ark look like a toy.

And Bantu and his family learned how to live side by side with the wild animals they brought into Bantu House. They took great pleasure in observing their wild habits, made easy game of appealing ones, and stayed away and safe from the dangerous ones.

But one hot afternoon, a school of hungry crocodiles disrupted the peace and harmony of Bantu House and totally altered its future and that of all its occupants. They broke out of their rooms and crawled into the Cabora Bassa pool where they found Bantu and his wife, Zanji, refreshing in its cool waters, instantly attacked them and savagely ate them up.

The Bantu children were totally devastated. They had been orphaned at a very young age when they still needed their parents to fend for them. Overcome with despair and grief, they mourned their parents inconsolably—ruing their parents' decision to let wild animals into Bantu House, and cursing the animals for repaying their parents' adventurous hospitality with such monstrous savagery. In anguish they vowed to butcher the wild animals and rid Bantu House of all of them.

After their mourning period the Bantu orphans stuck to their vow and vengefully took to killing their animal co-habitants in large numbers. They poisoned and trapped to death thousands of crocodiles, hyenas, and many dangerous animals. Bantu House became a huge slaughter house.

But this, which Bantu orphans, began as a mere act of retribution on the poor animals to avenge the tragic death of their parents, unexpectedly landed them into lucrative business. As Bantu House littered with carcasses of thousands of wild animals, their neighbours began to flock in to buy them up for their meat, ivory and animal skin supplies. Within a short period following the death of their parents, the Bantu orphans considerably amassed their own wealth from the sale of wild meat, animal skins, and ivory.

For many years on end the Bantu orphans thrived and basked in their new found wealth. This healed the great loss they suffered at the death of their parents. On the other hand, it also began to inspire romantic needs in them. They all began to actively seek and court intimate partners with whom to start their own respective families in the affluence of Bantu House.

Nkhosi being the eldest of them all, married first. Apao, their only sister, followed. Then Uhuru, and finally, Nzika, the last born.

But while the brothers did not mind the social status of the women they brought into Bantu House as their wives, they, especially Nkhosi who had firmly assumed the role of leader and monitor of all Bantu House affairs, took issue with Apao's choice of a husband. Apao got married to a well-travelled but poor man called Anzeru. Anzeru was from a distant, poor Mzansi village. Nkhosi and his younger brothers thought he had only come to live off their wealth and eventually siphon it off into his poor homeland.

They were totally wrong; in no time Anzeru introduced superior and more profitable ways of trade and industry in Bantu House. He had the crocodile skins which the Bantu orphans were selling fresh, and with many going to waste if not bought in time, tanned, made into lovely crocodile leather belts, bags, coats, hats, and shoes and sold as finished products. He had the elephant tusks worked into fine, expensive ivory plates, spoons, bungles, and ornaments. This brought him and his wife, Apao, and indeed all the Bantus greater fame and fortune. They all now became famous not only for their golden treasure-villa and plentiful supplies of wild meat, animal skins, and elephant tusks but also for their prized crocodile leather products.To both outsiders and the Bantus, Anzeru, the architect of all this transformation, was the man of Bantu House.

Unfortunately, this annoyed Nkhosi. He resented Anzeru's growing reputation. He felt it was overshadowing his role as the head of Bantu House and increasingly negating his leadership.

So one day, in a bid to clip Anzeru's wings, Nkhosi summoned his siblings and in-laws to his quarters.

"I would like to set something straight, " he announced.

"I am the leader of this entire estate and no other. I've seen you all freely trading and growing rich when some of you just a couple of years ago were as poor and bare as a goat's knee. No one should undertake any business or conduct any affair in this house without my authority. I am in-charge of all the resources in this estate you're using in your businesses. And after me come my brothers; after them, my sister, Apao; and after her, my children; and then, their cousins, my brothers' children. So you, Anzeru, for all your enterprise, you are under our authority like our wives here. "

To make sure that Anzeru was effectively brought under control, Nkhosi ordered him to start paying homage to them, the Bantus:

"Furthermore, " he said, *"Anzeru you found this house already built. You and anyone else who is going to marry into our family will at least pay for its maintenance by surrendering to us half of all your proceeds from your businesses in this estate. "*

Anzeru agreed.

Many years later an overseas stranger came to Bantu House. He came with hundreds of porters from neighbouring Mzansi villages bearing his visibly, heavy luggage. He spoke a foreign language, which none of the Bantus understood, and for that they called him Mlendo.

But Anzeru having been well-travelled himself, not only understood Mlendo's language but the destructive habits of overseas travellers like him. He, therefore, advised his in-laws against dealing with Mlendo.

Nkhosi, however, considered this advice as Anzeru's ploy for keeping him and his siblings away from Mlendo so that he alone who spoke his language could do business with him. Thus he contemptuously dismissed Anzeru's advice, ordered him to instead stay away from Mlendo, and elected Mlendo's own porters to interpret for them whatever their master said and wanted.

The porters told the Bantus that Mlendo was a merchant from Ulaya looking for builders who would build in Ulaya a remarkable villa such as theirs.

Although the actual builders of Bantu House were no longer around, Nkhosi saw in Mlendo's quest an opportunity for getting rid of his disconcertingly resourceful brother-in-law, Anzeru, together with his equally gifted children who made his own children look like prize retards. Thus he lied to Mlendo that his own brother-in-law and nephews, Anzeru and his sons, were excellent builders who would easily build him a replica of Bantu House in Ulaya. *"But for what would I let you have my best builders?"* Nkhosi pressed.

Mlendo asked his porters to bring out from his luggage a hand-held long machine.

"*What's this?*" enquired Nkhosi upon seeing it.

"*This is a gun,*" replied Mlendo, "*a machine we use back home to fell big animals with ease. I'll let you have it for your best builders.*"

"*It looks simple for that; how does it work?*"

"*I'll show you; but what's the biggest animal around here?*"

"*Oh, they are many. We've crocodiles, buffaloes, hippos, rhinos, elephants—but the elephants are the biggest of them all; and they aren't even outside this very house. Our father was very adventurous a long time ago. After building this house he let in all sorts of animals, and since his death we've struggled to get rid of them to create room for our growing families.*"

"*Then take me to the elephants, I show you what this machine can do even to the biggest of your animals.*"

Nkhosi led Mlendo, his porters, and the Bantus to the animal apartments in Bantu House. They soon came upon an immense herd of elephants with enormous long tusks. Mlendo, who was a Catholic, crossed himself several times in utter disbelief at a sight of such an awesome herd of elephants. He knew he had just stumbled upon a fortune, for he had come to Bantu House for the ivory too. "*Now, I can show you how this machine works,*" he said anxiously.

He ordered everyone to stand behind him, took aim at one of the big elephants which were standing a stone's throw from them, pulled the trigger, and boom! There was a loud explosion of fire and smoke that sent the spectators behind him and the elephants ahead of him scampering in fright. But as the smoke and dust cleared and the spectators' panic eased, they saw a big bull elephant lying down in front of them. *"I got him!"* exclaimed Mlendo.

Nkhosi was extremely impressed with the machine. *"How many builders would you want for your amazing machine, my friend?"* he solicited.

"Well, I'm going to give you this gun complete with its ammunition, bullets, and a maintenance kit. I expect you to equally give me a complete workforce of builders so that my house would be built as easily and quickly as you will be felling your big elephants."

"No problem, my friend," Nkhosi snorted.

As planned, Nkhosi later ordered his brother-in-law, Anzeru, and his sons to accompany Mlendo to Ulaya in exchange for the gun. Anzeru, his wife, and their children broke into vehement remonstrations against this. They didn't want to leave Bantu House and have their flourishing businesses disrupted.

But Nkhosi remained resolute. He went on to get the gun, ammunition, bullets, and its maintenance kit from Mlendo and told him to get his brother-in-law and his children in any way he wanted them.

Mlendo ordered his porters to round up Anzeru and his children. But Anzeru and his children went into hiding in secluded rooms of Bantu House. When Mlendo complained to Nkhosi that their deal was going to fall through as the men he wanted had fled into hiding in his vast house, Nkhosi instructed his own sons, who knew every corner of Bantu House, to help Mlendo and his porters capture their uncle and cousins.

They succeeded. They had Anzeru and his sons all captured and thrown into dhows that eventually took them to Ulaya.

Apao, who was violently separated from her husband and children, mourned bitterly as though they had died. In anguish she stripped off her clothes and went into Nkhosi's apartments and wailed: *"Look my brother! This is all you have left me with. Our parents are dead and you've taken away my beloved husband and children; oh Nkhosi, my brother, is this how you are going to take care of us?"*

Confronted by Apao's nakedness and harrowing laments, Nkhosi, his wife, and children retreated to their inner rooms, unable to face the bare facts of their sister and aunt's predicament.

Apao then went to reproach her younger brothers, Uhuru and Nzika, and their children. *"And you, my younger brothers and your many sons,"* she moaned, *"You couldn't come to the rescue of my husband and children. With your indifference you too have had me ruined. Oh, my brothers, how will you make me forget the tragic death of our parents like this? But I've a warning for you, with my children gone; next Nkhosi and his children will turn to yours. They'll soon find reasons for equally taking your children out of this tragic house. And remain unsupportive to each other as you were to my family, you too will be left naked like me."*

Ashamed and remorseful, they too retreated to their inner rooms, leaving grief-stricken Apao to face her miseries alone.

But in Ulaya, Anzeru and his sons excelled at building Mlendo's mansion although it was not their line of work. Being industrious as they were, they took to building Mlendo's mansion with breathtaking ingenuity. To begin with, Mlendo did not have a large land where a Bantu-House-like mansion would have stood; so they decided to build it upwards. And into the clouds soared their iron and steel construction of Mlendo's mansion. Just as the golden Bantu House had astounded many, Mlendo's iron and steel skyscraper, that Anzeru and his sons constructed, awed many. And many Ulayans began to ask for Anzeru and his sons to build them theirs too.

As demand grew for the construction works of Anzeru and his sons, Mlendo, who was now a proud director of Anzeru & Sons construction works, and astute as ever, decided to cash in by sailing back to Mzansi and bring from there more Bantu builders. And this time he took with him many guns, their maintenance kits, and a lot of ammunition in readiness for a massive exchange for Bantu builders.

But when he arrived in Mzansi and at Bantu House, in particular, Nkhosi—perhaps raked by the guilty his distraught sister had successfully stirred in him—told him that he no longer had any more builders to exchange for any gun. He also poignantly told him that he didn't need any more of his guns because one of his sons had used the first he gave them to fell his own brother when they quarrelled over it. *"So I've since destroyed the deadly and divisive weapon you sold me, my friend,"* further disclosed Nkhosi. *"And I don't want any more from you because they could finish my children."*

But Mlendo was in no mood to take 'No' for an answer, especially when he considered the fortune Anzeru and his sons

11

were bringing him back in Ulaya. He made as if he was leaving Bantu House having been turned down but instead secretly went to the apartments of Nkhosi's sons themselves whom their father was trying to protect from his guns and who on his first trip had helped him and his porters capture Anzeru and his sons. *"Your old father is losing his business sense and, indeed, his mind all together,"* he told them. *"To begin with, how could he destroy such an expensive machine I brought your household last time? Then he's refusing to have many more I've brought this time for similar trade. You must come to his aid, don't let his old brains ruin all of you."*

Mlendo won over Nkhosi's sons. They elected to deal with him behind their father's back. They accepted the guns and everything and settled on selling their remaining cousins, the Uhurus and Nzikas, who, incidentally, had already united against them for what they considered being overtaxed and taxed at all by the Nkhosis as if Bantu was not their grandfather too.

But capturing the Uhurus and Nzikas proved a bloody affair. As already stated, they presented a formidable combined force than that of the Anzerus. When Mlendo's porters came upon them and attempted to round them up, the Uhurus and Nzikas realized that the Nkhosis had equally sold them—as Apao, their aunt, had warned—and they quickly galvanized themselves into combat. And Apao, their aggrieved aunt herself, spurred them on. She told them that failure to defend themselves would see them all captured like her husband and sons. Thus seeing that the Uhurus and Nzikas were putting up a spirited fight to defend themselves, Mlendo ordered his porters to use the very guns he had brought for trade to break their resistance. Consequently, many Uhurus and Nzikas were slain, many, maimed and many more, ended up captured. The few who survived retreated into far flung rooms of Bantu House.

Mlendo was not pleased. He told the Nkhosis that the few Uhurus and Nzikas he had managed to capture were not enough value for the many guns he was going to leave them. So, to make up, he asked for many elephants to be felled so that he could instead get their tusks. The Nkhosis consented to this. And thousands of elephants were subsequently felled for their tusks.

Eventually Mlendo left Bantu House with dhows laden with elephant tusks and a number of Uhurus and Nzikas.

In Ulaya the tusks too proved big business as Mlendo's compatriots made all sorts of wonderful household items from them. This drove Mlendo to make several trips to Mzansi and Bantu House, in particular, to fell thousands and thousands of elephants for their tusks—so much so that even their population in Bantu House dwindled drastically.

Yet for his entire obsession with elephant tusks, Mlendo and his men never stopped to have the Uhurus and Nzikas captured whenever they encountered them in their remote hideouts as they went about hunting for the dwindling elephants. It was only when the elephant stocks had depleted considerably in Bantu House and the Uhurus and Nzikas continued proving difficult to capture, that he turned away from Bantu House and began trading with other houses in Mzansi even though they were smaller than Bantu House.

Abandoned by Mlendo and not given to industry as was Anzeru and his sons, the Nkhosis began to find it difficult to thrive. So it was that one day, as Mlendo was in Mzansi, Nkhosi desperately instructed his sons to pull down some of the golden walls of Bantu House and try to see if Mlendo would be interested in buying the golden bricks, thus released, for his own buildings in Ulaya.

When Mlendo came over, he instantly took to the golden bricks. But he advised that he was going to need a substantial amount of them if he was going to use them to build houses in his homeland. And excitedly, Nkhosi told him not to worry about that. He assured him that his sons were going to work flat out to pull down the unwanted walls of Bantu House, so much so that he would forever find golden bricks waiting to be ferried away.

Trade in Bantu House golden bricks between the Nkhosis and Mlendo boomed.

Not long after, Mlendo was joined in this booming trade with the Nkhosis by several of his competing compatriots. They also wanted to cash in on the Nkhosis' recklessness of trading off their priceless Bantu House golden bricks. And as competition intensified between Mlendo and his compatriots, the Nkhosis were worked into a frenzy of pulling down the walls of much of their famous Bantu House. In places where they had carelessly pulled down the walls, the roof almost caved in on them.

Afraid of ending up entombing themselves, Nkhosi instructed his sons to instead go and pull down the walls of the apartments where the Uhurus and Nzikas had fled into. And here they threw all caution to the wind; they wildly and mindlessly pulled down the walls like a pack of crazed vandals.

Often the rabid Nkhosi demolition squads violently broke

upon the Uhurus and Nzikas who then fled farther away leaving behind their possessions, much to their delight as they eagerly looted their cousins' possessions. But on numerous occasions before the Uhurus and Nzikas could even flee to safety, some viciously demolished sections of their apartments would abruptly cave in on them and kill them instantly. This increasingly rendered the Uhurus and Nzikas an endangered people.

The sorrowful plight of the Uhurus and Nzikas moved one of Mlendo's compatriots and competitor, Anansi, to come to their aid. Anansi armed his porters and the Uhurus and Nzikas themselves with guns to mount their defence and, indeed, that of their apartments and possessions in Bantu House.

Faced with this resistance, Nkhosi sold to Mlendo the entire half of Bantu House which Anansi and his porters and the Uhurus and Nzikas were successfully defending. He sold it for bales of cloth, as he was still opposed to guns. But when Mlendo tried to move in and take over this part of Bantu House, he was stopped by Anansi and his porters who had equally taken residence there. In view of the persistent attacks they had suffered at the hands of the Nkhosis, the Uhurus and Nzikas had asked Anansi and his porters to move in with them and offer them constant protection. And Anansi and his porters had firmly taken charge of the security and administration of this entire half of Bantu House where they resided with the Uhurus and Nzikas.

A bitter wrangle ensued between Mlendo and Anansi over this part of Bantu House as both claimed to have been given the right of occupation by its rightful owners. And seeing that the wrangle was likely to bring them into physical confrontation far away from their own homeland, they both decided to have the matter resolved by their courts of law in Ulaya.

The courts ruled in favour of Anansi. They said since Anansi had been granted residence by the Uhurus and Nzikas, who were the actual occupants of the disputed part of the house, he had every reason to be there. And Mlendo who was fraudulently sold this part of the house by the Nkhosis who were not its substantive occupants, they said had no business in it. They advised him to instead take up residence with the Nkhosis themselves, who took his bales of cloth, into their part of Bantu House.

Both Mlendo and Anansi abided by their court's ruling. Undeterred by the prospect of ruining a long cordial relationship he had established with the Nkhosis, Mlendo audaciously moved into their part of Bantu House. And instead of seeking to peacefully co-exist with them, he declared that the Nkhosis had forfeited their part of Bantu House to him because of the fraudulent manner in which they got his bales of cloth. And if they had to continue living with him in what until now was their house, they, he told them, had to do so only as his tenants who would be paying him rent.

Helpless, the Nkhosis succumbed.

Meanwhile, in the other half of Bantu House Anansi amiably embarked on teaching the Uhurus and Nzikas how to effectively manage their estate. In return, the Uhurus and Nzikas allowed Anansi the use of many resources in their estate. And Anansi who arrived in Bantu House as a struggling merchant, who was always upstaged by the long established Mlendo, rapidly grew wealthy. Unfortunately, this wealth, instead of cementing the mutually beneficial relationship between Anansi and the Uhurus and Nzikas, it would drive a hateful wedge of discord between them.

Anansi treated the wealth he made in Bantu House as the price the Uhurus and Nzikas were paying him for protecting them from their assailants. Despite his superb knowledge in estate management, he refused to commit any substantial amount of it to the rebuilding of the dilapidated part of their Bantu House. Save a very small amount of it he used to only rehabilitate his own apartment, he sent the rest of it to his homeland in Ulaya where he was having his own skyscraper constructed to rival those of Mlendo.

This exploitative tendency of Anansi brought him on a collision course with the Uhurus and Nzikas. They told him they would be better off managing their estate alone than with a negligent and exploitative mentor that he had become who only wanted to feather his own nest. Thus, they asked him to leave Bantu House.

When Anansi reminded the Uhurus and Nzikas that he was in Bantu House to protect them from Mlendo, who had now reduced their cousins, the Nkhosis, to utter slaves in their own house, they told him they were now capable of not only defending themselves against Mlendo but also emancipating the Nkhosis from his subjugation by equally expelling him from Bantu House.

After a long dispute characterized by an exchange of many bitter words and ugly actions, Anansi gave up. He surrendered all the keys he had to that part of Bantu House to the Uhurus, who were a more senior clan than the Nzikas, and left.

Having taken charge of their entire half of Bantu House, the Uhurus wasted no time to honour the pledge both they and the

Nzikas made to Anansi that they would equally emancipate their cousins, the Nkhosis, from Mlendo's control. They ordered Mlendo to take the cue from Anansi and leave Bantu House as well.

But Mlendo resisted leaving. He said unlike Anansi, he had bought his part of Bantu House from the Nkhosis.

Emboldened by their own successful expulsion of Anansi from Bantu House, the Uhurus whipped up the Nkhosis to rise against Mlendo whom they said was not only exploiting them but had no moral right to occupy any part of Bantu House with or without the bales of cloth he paid the Nkhosis. And the Nkhosis duly rose against Mlendo and made his continued stay in Bantu House untenable.

But unwilling to go without a fight, and being given to gun-fighting as he was, Mlendo declared war on all the Bantus. He recruited mercenaries from neighbouring Mzansi houses to fight the Bantus on the pretext that he was defending his property, Bantu House.

Still, the Bantus beat Mlendo and his mercenaries to it. Knowing all the corners of Bantu House as they did, they blocked all the vital passageways of the House with huge boulders, barricaded doorways of many apartments with heavy logs and with any missile they could lay their hands on, assailed entrapped Mlendo and his mercenaries from their vantage positions.

In May 1994, Mlendo conceded defeat and surrendered the keys he had to Bantu House to the Nkhosis.

Since then both the Uhurus and the Nkhosis have happily kept their own keys to Bantu House. But the Nzikas are terribly aggrieved by this whole arrangement. The Uhurus and Nkhosis have been keeping the keys to Bantu House to their exclusion. Whenever they are in need of the keys to both Bantu House and, indeed, their apartments, the Uhurus and Nkhosis do not readily give them the keys. They, the Uhurus and Nkhosis, claim busy work schedules and heavy administrative responsibilities prevent them from doing so. And a few Nzikas who have succeeded to have the keys, at least to their apartments, had to resort to corrupting, hustling, and hoodwinking the Uhurus and Nkhosis. But, the huge majority of them who cannot afford this have succumbed to miserable nights in the cold. For many years now they have failed to access their own apartments, let alone, their belongings therein. They have slept hungry and cold in the verandas, and corridors of their own House. And what hurts them most is that there are reports, and, indeed, irrefutable evidence, that the Uhurus and Nkhosis are readily and quickly giving the same keys to their apartments they deny them to total strangers who at the end of the day make away with many of their valuables. And this has left many of them mournfully concluded, and rightly so, that it is far much easier for total strangers to enter their apartments than it is for them.

But today, as I was about to embark on explaining this historical parable to my Facebook friends in a post, one of them, Omemeza, a Nzika himself, messaged me:

The long marginalized Nzikas of all persuasion have risen against their selfish cousins, the Uhurus and Nkhosis. All last night instead of retiring to our usual troubled sleep in the verandas and corridors of BantuHouse, Nzika rights activists kept us awake with drills in wresting the long sought after keys to our apartments from our cousins. And since the early hours of today we've—Arab-Spring-style—taken total control of all of Bantu House verandas, corridors, and doorways. We've entrapped our cousins in their apartments the way our forefathers had Mlendo and his mercenaries entrapped in Bantu House 50 years ago. The plan is to force them to surrender the keys to our apartments.

I quickly replied: *"What if they don't yield? They are notoriously stubborn."*

Omemeza replied back:

Nzika rights activists have taken that into consideration too and they equally have a contingency measure. If, as always, the Nkhosis and Uhurus will refuse to hand us the keys to our apartments, Nzika rights activists say we'll pull down the entire dilapidated BantuHouse, with our stubborn cousins entrapped in their apartments, just like the Nkhosis themselves did to our **forefathers a century ago.**

I again quickly put it to Omemeza that then that would be more senselessly catastrophic than all that has transpired in Bantu House before.

He objected:

Not really. Nzika rights activists have everything thought through; unlike the Nkhosis who pulled down the walls of Bantu House and recklessly sold its golden bricks to foreigners, Nzika rights activists are proposing a novel plan of using the golden bricks to construct a golden Berlin-wall-type high wall around the entire Bantu estate.

I couldn't help but instantly scoff at that: *"In this day and age that's rather retrogressive. The erection of Berlin-walls belongs to a chilly cold past."*

Fired up as though he was a Nzika rights activist himself, Omemeza countered:

Unlike the Berlin wall that kept the Germans apart, the Bantu golden wall will keep all Bantus together and inside but foreigners. It will be raised against foreigners who have been entering Bantu House illegally through ugly holes all around its old walls and end up making away with our many valuables.

Still finding Omemeza's passionate arguments out of place and rather tainted with xenophobic sentiment, I simply posted back: *"We now all live in one global village."*

He reposted:

Carefully analyse your words. You have just written 'one global village' and not 'one global house.' That still leaves all of us with a responsibility we cannot shirk: to put our respective houses in order in this 'one global village' of ours. The Ulayans are doing just that; and we, the Bantus, will be no exception. All other peoples wanting to deal with us simply have to be made to pass through designated steel gates of our golden wall where they will be properly screened when entering and leaving. Period!

I too left it at that and went on to explain the parable of Bantu orphans to all my Facebook friends and groups, but now with Omemeza's views in mind.

1

Not So Happy

A 50th Liberation Anniversary

An ill wind has blown me across the face of Africa. I have seen the poverty of Orlando East and the wealth of Morningside in Johannesburg. In Lusaka, I have seen the poor of Kanyama Township and the prosperous residents of Kabulonga... I have seen the faces of the poor in Mbari in Harare and the quiet wealth of Borrodale.

*And I have heard the stories of how those who had access to power, or access to those who had access to power, of how they have robbed and pillaged and broken all laws and all **ethical** norms with great abandon to acquire wealth....*

—Thabo Mbeki

Bantu African leaders and their families, colleagues, and elite circle of friends are like jewellery and make-up on a battered, bloody, and tear-stained face. They go about their activities clad in extravagant, expensive suits; they ride state of the art vehicles worth billions of dollars; and they live it up in massive treasure-troves of houses. And for all this they award themselves hefty salaries and allowances. For them, fifty years of African liberation is indeed worthy celebrating. They have bloomed and blossomed year in and year out. Year in and year out for fifty solid years now they, and only they, have thrived and flourished in Bantu Africa. But millions of ordinary Bantu Africans whose lives they purport to better flounder and founder in poverty. For fifty years now ordinary Bantu Africans have been systematically unemployed despite loads and loads of work waiting to be done to develop Bantu Africa. Their entrepreneurial spirit is punished by bribes to greedy immigration officers, policemen, council workers, and many such government or public service providers. Their agricultural ventures are under pain of perpetual ill reward. As for the vast mineral wealth under their feet, they have no means to exploit it. The banks say they are not credit-worthy, for they have nothing to their names—they are worthless nonentities. Despite inhabiting Bantu Africa for thousands of years now, they are just squatters, and the houses they have struggled to construct for themselves, are illegal structures that do not pass for collateral before the banks. But foreigners, Europeans and Asians, who came to Bantu Africa yesterday now own vast swaths of Bantu African land, and on the basis of that land ownership Banks entrust them with loads of money to put up mighty companies. And it's to them that poor ordinary Bantu Africans turn to offer their cheap labour—so meagre are the wages of their labour that they cannot feed, clothe, shelter or educate themselves, neither can they save themselves from ill health, and, let alone, bury themselves when they die.

Today, 25 May, 2012, as Bantu African elites were deservedly commemorating the liberation of Africa from European subjugation (congratulating and honouring each other with grand national awards for whatever individual roles they are said to have played in the ever so hyped up African liberation) tens of millions of Bantu Africans were struggling, to no avail, to shake out of the clutches of crushing poverty.

In Bantu African cities, with their allure of prosperity, emanating from imposing residences, shopping malls, and sky-scraping business houses patronized by a handful of hefty-salaried Bantu African elites, thousands of Bantu Africans, having succumbed to malaria, cholera, dysentery, tuberculosis, and AIDS, endemic in their overpopulated slums, were dragging their undernourished, aching skeletal bodies out of their damp, leaking shacks to go and seek medical attention in equally poorly run health centres and hospitals, where health workers supplement their meagre salaries with selling all essential drugs to bogus drug stores and see off their patients with mere prescriptions on rough pieces of paper; thousands more were leaving their pathetic slums for equally pathetic run-down market places, which reek of mounds of uncollected rotten garbage, dirty water from fish and meat stalls in blocked drainages, and human excreta from disused, faeces-strewn toilets, to vend second hand wares and all sorts of cheap Chinese products and to push purposefully king-sized car-wheeled wheel-barrows over laden with bales and bags of merchandise (grain, animal feed, dried fish, second hand clothes, etc.) for numerous struggling Bantu African small traders; thousands more were already slogging away at hard, health impairing, and poor paying jobs in Chinese, Indian, and government factories—all in a bid to survive just this day with a little relief from endless pain and despair.

Away from city shacks, mansions, malls and skyscrapers and the outrageous false glamour about them, 25 May, 2012 found over 200 million Bantu Africans, who, like their forefathers, have been abandoned to the miseries of dawn-to-dusk and soul-destroying back-breaking peasantry, heartbroken.. International cotton ginners operating in Bantu Africa had declared that they were going to buy their cotton at half the previous year's price. This entailed that all what they had worked for in the entire year would come to nothing as whatever portion of the money they would get for their cotton would again be taken away by the same international cotton companies as loan recoveries for cotton seeds, pesticides, sprayers, etc., they got from them to produce the cotton. Conversely, this meant widespread hunger among rural Bantu African communities—most of them had banked on buying food with money from their cotton sales. It also meant many rural Bantu Africans going about in the same old tattered clothes and their children sleeping in jute sacks for blankets. This in turn meant no business for local traders who largely sell their merchandise to farmers. Then it spelt the end of school for most children, as their parents would fail to pay their school fees. Ultimately it condemned both young and old in rural Bantu Africa to untimely deaths from curable diseases such as malaria, as there would be no money to buy medicines, which medical workers prescribe to patients.

In Zambia, for example, some farmers opted to burn several tons of cotton in anger rather than let cotton companies take it away for a song. The Patriotic Front (PF) government, which came to power promising that it would put *"more money"* in Zambians' pockets, announced to the nation that it could not do anything to help poor farmers out of their predicament. And the Zambia National Farmers Union summed it all up that the poor farmers were *"on their own."*

Thus, over 200 million Bantu Africans were helplessly cast a year back into grinding poverty—and so much for the UN's Millennium Development Goals (MDGs) forecasting poverty reduction in Africa by the year 2015.

The truth is no amount of years of political independence and well-meaning time-frames on tackling poverty will see the majority of Bantu Africans out of poverty. European subjugation of Bantu Africans, as we shall see in detail later, was never the cause of Bantu African poverty. It was, in fact, prompted and abetted by Bantu African poverty itself. It came and thrived on Bantu African poverty and 50 years ago it left it all the more acute and deplorable. In no way is this to imply that the majority of Bantu African poor will always be with us. Indeed, poverty in Bantu Africa is ancient—it goes back far beyond the European subjugation of Bantu Africans—but there still was a time when the majority of Bantu Africans were affluent. And that's where our hope lies—Bantu African poverty may be ancient but it is certainly not inherent in the majority of Bantu Africans. Whatever brought it about is foreign and, of necessity, carries the seed of its undoing, as that which is begun or brought about can be brought to an end or taken away.

Many peoples the world over rely on their written word to tell and retell their histories. But in Bantu Africa, our history was passed from one generation to the other through oral narratives. Obviously this is not a very reliable way. But where in doubt we have let our long dead ancient narrators be exhumed and made to retell their stories. And from Tshikapa archaeological site in the Congo to Zambia's Machili, Lusu, Kalambo falls, Kalomo, Kalundu, Isamu Pati, Kangila, Ing'ombe Ilede, and Dambwa; and Malawi's Mwanasapa, Mbande Hill, Kapeni Hill, Nyika Plateau, and Nkhope bay; and Zimbabwe's Gokomere, Ziwa, Mabveni, and the famous Great Zimbabwe, to name but a few—the long dead ancient Bantu African narrators have been exhumed and made to retell amazing stories of widespread wealth and affluence in Bantu Africa in the days of their lives. Yes, subjecting Bantu African remains from various historical sites throughout Bantu Africa to radio carbon tests indicate that by A.D. 100 Bantu Africans were already an effective iron, copper, and bronze economy. In their book, *From Iron Age to Independence, A History of Central Africa,* D.E. Needham, E.K. Mashingaidze, and N. Bhebe state:

The coming of the knowledge of iron-working to Central Africa is closely associated with the early pastoral and crop cultivating settlers. These mixed farmers built large settlements or villages consisting of huts made of poles and mud, and hardened floors. The huts had thatched roofs and were similar to the huts built by modern Bantus of Central Africa. The period from about the second to the tenth centuries seems to have witnessed [these] Early Iron Age occupations, especially in Zambia, Malawi, and Zimbabwe.

And in its segment of Bantu African history, the *New Basic*

Education Resource Atlas for Zambia recounts that:

When the Bantu-speaking peoples discovered how to [process] iron, they made tools that helped to improve their methods of farming and clearing forests. The Bantu-speaking peoples grew in number and many travelled in search of farming land and pasture.

Indeed, the use of iron, bronze, and copper products not only made Bantu Africans better farmers, but also increased their general economic output as it were—year by year, decade by decade, and century by century they became more innovative and industrious. They manufactured tools and sculptured historic and priceless artefacts which even today decorate numerous museums throughout the world. From chosen tree barks and grasses they weaved baskets, mats, hats, and fabrics for both domestic and commercial purposes. That they were proverbial hunters is stuff for primary school education, but using iron and copper tools they worked various animal skins and horns into fine, expensive products—ivory bracelets, cups, plates, spoons, cultural ornaments, and leather coats, bags, hats, shields, ropes, shoes, and many more. When the Chinese and Arabs came to Bantu Africa and saw these products, lucrative trade between them and Bantu Africans ensued. Archaeological excavations in numerous burial sites across Bantu Africa and subsequent radio carbon tests on overwhelming amounts of excavated Bantu African, Chinese, and Arab products—Bantu African hoe-heads, hammerheads, sheaves of copper wire, ivory bungles, rows of copper bungles, gold objects, bronze and clay pots, and Chinese/Arab vessels, bowls, coloured glass beads, and cowries shells: —dating from the 10th to the 12th centuries—mean only one thing.: Bantu Africa witnessed flourishing economic activities from the 10th to the 12th centuries.

Of course, then there were no iron-roofed houses, piped water, cars, planes, electricity via copper wires, radios, TVs, computers, and all the wonderful high-tech gadgets of the modern world. But none of these will ever replace and surpass the gratification Bantu Africans derived from their economic activities which were centred on their fauna and flora, and rooted in their plateaus and plains, and sustained by their rivers and lakes. With animal hunting and leather tanning and dyeing, and carving, sculpturing, and weaving, and iron and copper processing, and animal rearing and cereal production, Bantu Africans, then, in all truthfulness, knew no unemployment, poverty, and misery.

That such widespread prosperity in Bantu Africa was later followed by a whole millennium of pervasive poverty, something deeply insidious set into the flourishing 10th- 12th century Bantu African economy: *AVARICE.* A few individuals and groups among Bantu Africans themselves sought to gain mastery and power over others to take over the flourishing Bantu African economy. D.E. Needham, E.K. Mashingaidze, and N. Bhebe in *From Iron Age to Independence, A History of Central Africa* put this rather approvingly—and this as well demonstrates how insidious what set into Bantu Africans' economic life was and still is:

As [Bantu African] communities became larger numerically, and as more people became involved in a greater variety of

economic activities, more effective systems of governing
communities were required to replace family or village heads.
Men of greater power and authority rose to prominence and in
most cases these men were respected and even feared....

The power and mastery that begun to obtain in Bantu Africa
by, say, the 12th century blighted the entire flourishing Bantu
African economy. It impoverished the vast majorities of Bantu
Africans, eliminating them from the mainstream of Bantu
African economic activities. The few powerful individuals and
groups that emerged subjected all other Bantu Africans to
plunder, conquests, and systematic laws of deprivation to gain
mastery over them and take over the flourishing Bantu African
economy. Certainly, if this ruinous ascendancy to power and
mastery in Bantu Africa was consigned to only one or a few
centuries, Bantu Africans would have recovered from it and
gone on to stage a European-style renaissance that would have
ushered in a new, vibrant Bantu African economy. But for about
1000 years, that is from around the 12th century up to this very
century, 21st century, power and mastery in Bantu Africa has
been, and still is, achieved at the expense of the great majority
of Bantu Africans. And thus Thabo Mbeki, the illustrious South
African thinker and former President was compelled to
denounce Bantu African power and those who seek it. In his
2001 newspaper feature entitled '*African Renaissance*,' Mbeki,
never mind he was then himself serving as South African
President, railed:

They seek access to power or access to those who have power so
that they can corrupt the political order for personal gain at all

costs. In this equation, the poverty of the masses of the people becomes a necessary condition for the enrichment of the few and the corruption of political power the only possible condition for its exercise.

It is out of this pungent mixture of greed, dehumanizing poverty, obscene wealth, and endemic public and private corrupt practice that many of Africa's coups d'état, civil wars, and situations of instability are born and entrenched.

And so it has been for about 1000 years now. When 1000 years or so ago shrewd and greedy Bantu Africans sought power and control, they rose raiding and conquering bands who they paid with loot from their plunder. And for the loot, a reward too appealing for many a young and able-bodied Bantu African to decline then, hordes and hordes of raiding Bantu Africans wreaked havoc on entire Bantu African populations. Many Bantu Africans were slaughtered, their houses and whole villages, ransacked; their tools and many valuable household possessions, looted; their cattle, goats, pigs, birds, and cereals, taken; their gardens and fields of crops, seized; and those who ended up taken captive, especially women and girls, were stripped of all their freedom—they were raped and forced into polygamous marriages and made to toil for their captors. The raiders exulted in all these spoils of their plunder and their masters revelled in presiding over it all, so much so that they even proudly took up monstrous titles—Mwata Yamvo (Lord of the Vipers or Master of Wealth) was the title of Bantu Africa's 13th century Lunda Empire ruler in Central Africa while Mwene Mutapa (Master Pillager) was the title of Bantu Africa's 14th century ruler of the Mwene Mutapa Empire in Southern Africa.

This culminated in a long chain of civil unrest, famines, poverty, and misery in Bantu Africa.

For many today, the catastrophic raids and plunder that swept through all of Bantu Africa and shaped the destiny of Bantu Africans in the last millennium are simply noted as conquests of one weaker Bantu African group by another mightier one. And the resultant empires and kingdoms which the 'mightier' Bantu African groups established in the process are saluted. The Luba-Lunda Empire in Central Africa, the Mwene Mutapa Empire in Southern Africa, and the Kongo Kingdom in South West Africa are all cited with acclaim by many scholars. And there are volumes upon volumes of the glowing history of these Bantu African empires and kingdoms. But hugely overlooked is the millennium-long tragedy of ordinary Bantu Africans at whose expense they were established.

2

Centuries

Of

Deprivation and Devastation

At least fifteen million Africans were forcibly transported across the Atlantic during the period of the slave-trade, the numbers increasing steadily throughout that period, reaching a maximum of 100,000 a year in the first decades of the nineteenth century. In addition, an equal number probably died during the Atlantic crossings. Such a drain on the population could have only the most serious consequences for societies whose population was at that time neither large nor closely settled. Such impoverishment could not be balanced by any equivalent economic gain. In fact, the slave-trade ruined the cultures of the African groups, which procured slaves for the European slave-traders. Wars increased in number and destructiveness, they were fought for the purpose of taking captives, and to defend one's freedom and often one's life. The distance between rulers and their common subjects, who might at one time be sold, increased and became unbridgeable. Respect for life diminished and executions and cruel sacrifices increased.

—Jacques Maquet

From about the 14th century to the 19th, Bantu Africa saw intense establishments of large kingdoms and empires. And by the 16th century, the whole of it, from Central Africa to Southern Africa, was largely divided between the Luba-Lunda Empire in Central Africa, the Kongo Kingdom in South West Africa, and the Mwene Mutapa Empire in Southern Africa. Apart from having fierce autocratic rulers at the helm, these kingdoms and empires developed advanced systems of government and government structures which are not any different from modern Bantu African ones. Of the very first known Bantu African kingdoms, the Luba Kingdom, founded by one Kongolo through conquests of neighbouring independent Bantu African groups, D.E. Needham, E.K. Mashingaidze, and N. Bhebe in *From Iron Age to Independence, A History of Central Africa,* attest:

The process of state-building in Luba reached a very high degree during the Kunda period. Kala Ilunga and his successors tried to maintain a centralized administration in Luba. Thus the King presided over a very strong government because he was himself a powerful ruler. He assumed a new traditional title and was no longer known as Kongolo but as the Mulopwe. Under Kunda rule, the Mulopwe alone had the final word on matters of war, and he controlled external trade…

The Mulopwe had many officials and chiefs to help him running his government, who were officially called balopwe (the plural of Mulopwe). They lived at the king's court rather like government ministers and civil servants in a modern government. They were in charge of various departments and sections of Mulopwe's administration. The main department was the army and the police looking after order and peace as well as defending the kingdom from external forces…

The same can be said of the Kongo Kingdom in South West Africa and the Mwene Mutapa in Southern Africa. This was certainly the one and only age of real African empires and kingdoms. Bemoaning the disruption, the European slave-trade and imperialism caused to this developing Bantu African government system between the 16th and 18th century, the venerable historian of Africa, Basil Davidson (1914 – 2010), in his book, The Search for Africa, writes:

There is much to suggest that the modes of self-organization of Africans…had reached a point of growth where forms of large organizational change were in course, or at least in prospect. Kings in some regions acquired more power than before. Africans without kings developed new forms of central authority. Groups of neighbouring communities were perhaps on the verge of forming new constellations of multi-ethnic composition. As it was, there came instead the European intrusion, and the history of the Africans became, for a while, much more the history of the European.

However, subjected to an objective, critical analysis, a chilling fact emerges that even before they were disrupted by the European intrusion none of all those expanding and advancing Bantu African kingdoms and empires enhanced the lives of the majority of their people. Life for ordinary Bantu Africans in the Age of African Empires and Kingdoms was characterized by destitution and misery brought about by systematic deprivation and servitude at the hands of their emperors, kings, and royal establishments. In any case, the underlying cause for all the expansions and advancement of Bantu African kingdoms and empires was still to amass more and more wealth and power for the emperors, kings, and their courtiers at the expense of the great majority of Bantu Africans they subjugated, and never to enhance their lives.

Thus, if some conquered and dispossessed Bantu African group ended up in destitution, it did not concern Bantu African emperors, kings, and their courtiers as long as that group of people was alive to pay them tribute.

Mwata Yamvo (the Lord of Vipers or Master of Wealth), the Emperor of the Lunda Empire, a sister empire of the Luba Empire, had his empire organized and administered to thorough organization like any modern state be it in Africa or in the world. Throughout his vast empire, which at its height spread across much of modern Zambia, Angola, and the Democratic Republic of Congo, *"villages were grouped into administrative*

*districts each under an official known as the **kilolo**"[1] (To this
day a government minister is called a "kilolo" or a "chilolo" in*
several Bantu African languages in Zambia). But Mwata Yamvo
did not develop that sophistication in administration to the
extent of having *kilolos* in the far flung villages of his vast
empire out of concern for all his subjects' welfare. His *kilolos*
were more of tax hounds than civic leaders. They hounded area
chiefs and village headmen for tribute to him. In turn area chiefs
and village headmen compelled their subjects to surrender much
of the proceeds of their hunting, fishing, mining, ingenuity,
manufacturing, and, indeed, labour to Mwata Yamvo. Again
D.E. Needham, E.K. Mashingaidze, and N. Bhebe, in *From Iron
Age to Independence, A History of Central Africa,* observe:

*The larger the territory under the Mwata Yamvo's control the
better the trading, because chiefs in the conquered areas were
required to pay tribute in the form of ivory, copper, slaves, salt,
and labour. These goods were important in the Mwata Yamvo's
trade with the Portuguese and with the Swahili ports on the east
coast.*

But for all they gave up to their emperors and kings—ivory,
gold, copper, iron, tools, game meat, cattle, goats, pigs, cereals,
leather, mats, skills, labour, and, indeed, life—ordinary Bantu
Africans, be it in the Luba-Lunda Empire, the Kongo Kingdom,
or in the Mwene Mutapa Empire, received absolutely nothing in
return.Bantu African kings and emperors built no public roads,

---

[1] D.E. Needham, E.K. Mashingaidze, and N. Bhebe, *From Iron
Age to Independence, a History of Central Africa.*

schools, and health centres, nor did they provide any services to their subjects. On the other hand, they had built for themselves awesome historic capitals or courts where they lived lives of splendour. To this day massive stone ruins of the12th – 15th century Great Zimbabwe, the then mighty capital of the Mwene Mutapa Empire, which stretched from the Indian Ocean coast of Mozambique via all of modern Zimbabwe up to the Zambezi plains in the north (now southern and western parts of Zambia) and down to the Limpopo River in the south (the boundary of Zimbabwe, Botswana, and South Africa), still stand as testimony of the affluence Bantu African emperors, kings, and their courtiers enjoyed and the servitude their ordinary stone-hewing subjects suffered under them.

In the Age of African Empires and Kingdoms every facet of life revolved around the all-powerful emperors, kings, and their royal establishments. Nothing good ever happened in Bantu Africa without ending up to the exclusive enjoyment of Bantu African kings, emperors, and their establishments. And the biggest indictment against the Age of African Kingdoms and Empires is that affluence which before was widespread became a preserve of royalty. Unfortunately, and as if to prove that the chain of deprivation which this dark age set in motion in Bantu Africa around the 12th century is still running strong today in the 21st century, that same indictment still stands valid and accurate if made against current Bantu African governments and their civil service vis-à-vis the poverty of the great majority of their people. While the might and affluence of Mwata Yamvo's Lunda Empire, for instance, did not apply to ordinary Lunda subjects, reports of economic growth, let's say in Zambia, do not pertain to the ordinary Zambian citizens but to the tiny minority of those who happen to be in government and the civil service. Ordinary people in the Lunda Empire lived in abject slavery conditions and poverty just as they live in abject deprivation and poverty in Zambia today. Interestingly, and to stretch our comparison a little further, while the Lunda Emperor 500 years ago chose for himself the title of Mwata Yamvo (Lord of the Vipers), the current Zambian President, Michael Sata, chose for himself the nick name of "King Cobra," and even used to proudly display a huge, black toy-cobra in his office.

However, back then, ordinary Bantu Africans dared to stand up against the subjugation and dispossession they suffered at the hands of their kings, emperors, and royal establishments. They openly rebelled against the *kilolos* and the authority they represented and they connived with foreign merchants to trade secretly away from the prying eyes of the *kilolos*. Daredevil conspiracies and revolts against Bantu African monarchies spread rapidly. But at that point in time, $15^{th} - 16^{th}$ century, Bantu African monarchies and their establishments were far too strong for any of their subjects' subversive activities—be they foreign sponsored or not. Living true to his malicious title, and earning himself notoriety for cruelties that would chill Bantu Africa down the ages just at the mention of his name, Mwata Yamvo, for one, responded with severe brutality which set in motion one of the world's greatest human migrations of all time: the Luba-Lunda migrations which peopled much of Central and Southern Africa. Mwata Yamvo unleashed a spate of land, livestock, and material confiscations, torture, enslavement, and exterminations of Bantu African individuals and groups accused of connivance, conspiracy, and rebellion against his *kilolos* and monarchy at large.

Thus, fleeing perpetual deprivation and servitude and a relentless tyranny of land, livestock, and material confiscations, torture, enslavement, and exterminations, many Bantu Africans migrated far and away from their original kingdoms and empires to begin new lives either as independent communities or as small kingdoms or chiefdoms. Various modern day Bantu African groups such as the Luyi (Lozi), Lenje, Kasanje, Luvale, Bisa, Bemba, Chewa, Tumbuka, et cetera, were established either as independent ethnic groups or as small kingdoms during this time following these mass migrations.

But wherever the migrants went to settle, their new rulers knew no better ways of attaining themselves power and wealth than the appropriations and savagery of the kings and emperors they fled from. To expand and consolidate their small kingdoms, they too raised armies and raided neighbouring Bantu African groups who like them had just fled from the tyranny of their common parent empires. They too seized their neighbours' lands, livestock, household property, women, and banished, enslaved or butchered their men folk.

The Lozi under Litunga plundered and subjugated the Nkhoya and many smaller Bantu African groups of Western Zambia; the Chewa under Undi enslaved and exploited the Nsenga and other Bantu African groups in Eastern Zambia; the Bemba under Chitimukulu molested and ransacked the Lungu and Mambwe in Northern Zambia; the Yao under various chiefs attacked and oppressed the Tonga in Malawi; the Ndebele under Mzilikazi raided and displaced the Shona in Zimbabwe; and the Zulu under Shaka, with their *"mfecane"* wars (raiding wars) assailed and ravaged many surrounding Bantu African groups in South Africa. And from their own followers too, the new Bantu African rulers regularly demanded tribute in form of livestock, ivory, game meat, leather, gold, copper, iron, crafts, beautiful virgin girls and, indeed, anything that would please them. You only have to attend or watch on TV modern Bantu African traditional ceremonies to see a re-enactment of this.

So despite fleeing severe tyrannies of Bantu African kings and emperors, Bantu Africans never found respite under migrating chiefs. And when some of them tried to resist being further dispossessed and subjugated by these migrant chiefs, their lot was not any different than that of those who tried to resist or disobey the tyrannies of the Mwata Yamvos. Gruesome exterminations, like those carried out by King Shaka and his Zulu *impis* (warriors), atrocious land and livestock seizures, like those perpetrated by King Mzilikazi and his *Amajaha* (young warriors), and brutal and traumatizing hounding and driving of dissidents into slavery were migrant Bantu African rulers punishments of choice. And this was the ruthless and oppressive 16th – 19th century Bantu Africa Europeans found and aggravated.

Anti-European African liberation propaganda has left many believing that Europeans are chiefly to blame for the slavery that Africans suffered at their hands as though they came to Bantu Africa with their guns blazing and their whips cracking driving Bantu Africans into chains and yokes of slavery. No, Europeans found Bantu Africans already selling their supposed outlaws to Arab slave-traders who for hundreds of years before had been trading with Bantu Africans.

And who blames a hyena or a vulture for feasting on human remains. Owing to their opportunistic nature, Europeans only rose to the occasion to put to profitable use the Bantu African human resource they found, at most, being exterminated and, at least, sold to Arab slave-traders by Bantu African emperors, kings, and chiefs for subversion, rebellion, and disobedience. Their compatriots in Europe and the Americas had tea and sugar

plantations and newly acquired colonies such as Brazil in need
of labourers; and finding healthy, able-bodied Bantu Africans
being butchered was like nowadays finding crude oil being spilt.
Without wasting a tempo they offered to buy up the unwanted
Bantu Africans to go and sell them off at a profit to their
compatriots; and Bantu African rulers counting it all as good-
riddance, happily accepted the offer. And obviously thankful too
to those Europeans were the unwanted Bantu Africans
themselves who would have otherwise ended up exterminated.
And when all these factors are taken into perspective, there is
nothing comical at all with Africans in the Diaspora thanking
God, and more practically Europeans, for putting their ancestors
onto slavers. Entire African communities in the Americas and
the Caribbean—and what amazing personalities they have
turned out to be—would have been obliterated while still in the
loins of their unwanted ancestors at some Bantu African
extermination ground had it not been for European opportunism.

The first Europeans to come to Bantu Africa were the
Portuguese in the 15th century. Diego Cao (1452 -1488) was the
first European to set foot in Bantu Africa when he entered Bantu
Africa through the mouth of the Congo River in 1482. Then his
compatriot, Bartolommeo Diaz (1450 – 1500) reached the Cape
of Good Hope in 1488; and the most famous Portuguese
voyager of them all, Vasco da Gama (1460 – 1524) reached
Mozambique in 1497. But establishing political, social, and
economic relations with Bantu Africa then was not their real
interest. They, mostly, made stop-overs in Bantu Africa for
fresh supplies of food and water as they tried to explore around
it and discover sea routes to India; this is especially true for the
ambitious Vasco da Gama.

India then was many a sailor's and merchant's pilgrimage

because of its famous trade in spices—some of them, in a passionate attempt to get to India (and hence the name India), even ended up mistaking South America, which they accidentally reached, for India(and hence the name India, as in Red Indians and the West Indies, being associated with South America). However, when these explorers and their respective crews stepped on the shores of Bantu Africa, they quickly discovered that there was something much more to Bantu Africa than fresh supplies of food and water and even more precious than the Indian spices: Bantu African slaves, gold, and ivory. They found Bantu Africans trading in the much needed slaves, gold, and ivory and hankered to participate.

The distinguished Basil Davidson succinctly records this in his book, *Old Africa Rediscovered*:

They anchored in havens that were thick with ocean shipping. They went ashore to cities as fine as all but a few they could have known in Europe. They watched a flourishing maritime trade in gold and iron and ivory and tortoise shell, beads and copper and cotton cloth, slaves and porcelain; and saw that they had stumbled on a world of commerce even larger, and perhaps wealthier, than anything that Europe knew.

To these European sailors of the last years of the fifteenth century the coast of Eastern Africa could have seemed a great deal more civilized than their own coast of Portugal.

When Diego Cao, Bartolommeo Diaz, and Vasco da Gama and their respective men returned to Portugal and reported their amazing discoveries in Bantu Africa—Vasco da Gama even took Bantu African gold to their monarchy as tribute—their king and compatriots wasted no time to get involved in the flourishing Bantu African commerce they had coveted.

King Manuel I of Portugal (1469 – 1521) commissioned hundreds of sailors and merchants to voyage to Bantu Africa with shiploads of Portuguese merchandise, bidding to establish trade relations between Portugal and Bantu Africa. And by 1500 they were back on the shores of Bantu Africa courting its leading commercial empires, the Kongo Kingdom in South West Africa and the Mwene Mutapa Empire in Southern Africa.

In the Kongo Kingdom the Portuguese, much to their elation, were received with open arms. Not only did the Manikongo (King of Kongo), Nzingaà Nkuwu (14-- – 1506), and his royal establishment take to the Portuguese merchandise, but also to the Portuguese themselves—the Manikongo fell in love with the Portuguese at first sight. Their demeanour, workmanship (as displayed in the ships they came in), culture, language, and religion immensely captivated him. He immediately took up a Portuguese title of Joao I and had himself and his family baptized by the Portuguese into their Catholicism. Thus, he not only sought to be established between his Kingdom and Portugal trade relations but a cultural assimilation too. And this he promptly let his counterpart, King Manuel I, know. King Manuel I and the Portuguese jumped at this as they now knew that they were, in fact, going to reap their intended benefits in the Kongo Kingdom for nothing more than a song. On subsequent voyages to the Kongo Kingdom they sent the Manikongo and his people teachers and missionaries to start the work of assimilating them into Portuguese culture and converting many more of them to Catholicism. In addition to this, several promising young Kongos were taken to Portugal for detailed assimilation; and ambassadors were exchanged between Mbanza Kongo, the capital of the Kongo Kingdom, and Lisbon, the capital of Portugal. And for all this the Manikongo and the Kongo Kingdom paid the Portuguese in ivory, copper, and slaves.

To reap a fortune from Bantu Africa's gold, the Portuguese sailed to the leading Bantu African gold producing and trading empire, the Mwene Mutapa Empire. But unlike the Kongo Kingdom which had its capital easily accessible at Mbanza Kongo, about 150km from the coast, the Mwene Mutapa Empire, despite controlling the gold trade on its Mozambican coastal cities, had its capital deep in the near-impenetrable interior of Southern Africa at Great Zimbabwe, about 450km from the coast. This presented the Portuguese with a lot of problems in reaching the Emperor of the Mwene Mutapa Empire to try their cultural charm. Not for want of trying, the Portuguese sailors and merchants travelled by boats on the mighty Zambezi River to get to the Mwene Mutapa but they could only get as far as Tete, about 300km away from Great Zimbabwe. The hardships of travelling on the unknown river full of rapids as is the Zambezi River, tropical diseases such as malaria to which they had no immunity, and skirmishes with Bantu African groups living along the Zambezi River and with the Mwene Mutapa's own warriors stationed in Mozambique to defend that part of the empire—all prevented them from going any further. So they instead settled for meagre returns from the Mwene Mutapa dictated gold trade on the Mozambican coastal cities.

Nevertheless, the Portuguese remained steadfast to their faith in their cultural diplomacy which had worked for them so wonderfully in the Kongo Kingdom. They believed that if they could get to meet the Mwene Mutapa in person and affect their cultural charm on him, followed with a substantial amount of softening him up with their Catholic Christianity, their fortunes in this vast gold-rich empire would tremendously improve. To this end, they managed, against all odds, to have a Portuguese Jesuit missionary, Fr. Goncalo da Silveira worm up his way to the Mwene Mutapa in 1561. But despite succeeding to convert the Mwene Mutapa and his wife to Catholicism, Fr. Goncalo da Silveira could not win over the suspicious Mwene Mutapas for the Portuguese. Convinced that Fr. Goncalo was just a Portuguese agent sent to soften them up with Christianity in a bid to take over their empire, the Mwene Mutapas ditched his Catholic faith and had him executed.

Meanwhile, back in the Kongo Kingdom the Portuguese took to raking in staggering profits from the trade in Bantu African slaves. Overwhelming demand for Bantu African slaves had gripped the Americas, the Caribbean, and Europe. This invigorated the Portuguese to intensify their activities of securing Bantu African slaves in the Kongo Kingdom. Finding relying on the Manikongo to sell them his outlaws totally inadequate to meet the increasing demand for Bantu African slaves, they unscrupulously cast aside their friendship and Christian fellowship with him and his people and, only then, picked up arms and begun to indiscriminately hound down Bantu Africans and flog them into their slavers. And the slave-trade which had come as a redeeming deed for Bantu African outlaws who otherwise would have been exterminated by their rulers became the scourge of all Bantu Africans. The Portuguese now wanted every Bantu African—outlaw, loyalist, royalty, subject, man, woman, boy or girl—they could lay their hands on shackled in their slavers. Because they were too few in number to perpetrate such an enormity in the Kongo Kingdom, they enlisted rival Bantu African groups opposed to the Kongo Kingdom such as the Jaga to raid and capture their neighbours for them.

Betrayed and besieged by his beloved Portuguese, the Manikongo, Mvembaà Nzinga (c. 1456 – 1543) who succeeded his father, Nzinga à Nkuwu, upon his death in 1506 and who was christened Afonso at his baptism and hence his later title of King Afonso I, protested strongly against this unwarranted onslaught to his Portuguese counterpart King John III, who had succeeded King Manuel I in 1521.

In a letter written to King John III in 1526, the Manikongo Mvemba à Nzinga aka King Afonso I complained bitterly:

Each day the traders are kidnapping our people—children of this country, sons of our nobles and vassals, even people of our own family. This corruption and depravity are so widespread that our land is entirely depopulated.

We need in this Kingdom only priests and schoolteachers and no merchandise, unless it is wine and flour for mass. It is our wish that this Kingdom not be a place for the trade or transport of slaves.

But King John III simply ignored his counterpart's protests and instead sent more Portuguese slavers to the Kongo Kingdom.

Distraught, the Manikongo Mvemba à Nzinga, a well-educated, devout Catholic King, who might have thought

48

himself respected even in Rome, then wrote a letter to Pope Clement VII, reporting the Portuguese atrocities in his Catholic Kingdom and requesting him to intervene and order, in the name of God and the Catholic Church, King John III and the Portuguese to stop their savagery acts against a fellow Christian and Catholic Kingdom, but again it was to no avail.

In fact, to the Manikongo's dismay and disillusionment the Pope's own nuncios in the Kongo Kingdom, Portuguese Catholic priests, some of whom of no less an illustrious order than the Society of Jesus aka Jesuits to which the current Pope, Francis I, belonged, joined *"in the slave-trade and neglected the schools and church work."*[2](The Mwene Mutapa who had Fr. Goncalo da Silveira slain at Great Zimbabwe may just have guessed right.)

So unfettered by neither the Church that had proclaimed itself a force of good nor the Portuguese monarchy that had purported to advance civilization, the Portuguese in the Kongo Kingdom wrenched thousands and thousands of Bantu Africans into slavery to amass themselves astounding wealth.

And just as they had thought the wonderful success they had with their cultural charm in the Kongo Kingdom could be repeated in the Mwene Mutapa Empire to gain them control of the gold trade, the Portuguese now thought the brute force that had achieved them even more stupefying slave-trade proceeds in the Kongo Kingdom would equally wrest them the gold mines from the Mwene Mutapa. Consequently, in 1569 the King of Portugal, King Sebastian this time, sent a 1000-strong force to

---

[2] D.E. Needham, E.K. Mashingaidze, and N. Bhebe, *From Iron Age to Independence, a History of Central Africa.*

the Bantu African empire to try and conquer the stubborn—and as far as they were concerned, heathen and murderous—Mwene Mutapa.

But they were wrong again. Even the 1000-strong force which was led by the veteran Portuguese soldier and explorer in Francisco Barreto (1520 – 1573) whom King Sebastian presumptuously named *'Conqueror of the Mines,'* did not succeed due to similar obstacles as those faced by their compatriots who had tried to get to the Mwene Mutapa in the 1530s.

Tropical diseases and skirmishes with several Bantu African groups they encountered in Mozambique on their way to the Mwene Mutapa reduced Barreto's 1000 men to a mere 200 by 1573. The supposed *'Conqueror of the Mines'* himself, Francisco Barreto, fell ill and died on July 9,1573 at Sena, along the Zambezi River and about 100kms from Tete. Although King Sebastian later sent reinforcements, still they couldn't come to conquer the Mwene Mutapa and wrest the gold mines and trade from them.

Unfortunately, the repeated and costly failures by the Portuguese to secure control of Bantu African gold trade from the Mwene Mutapa rendered the slave-trade the only viable and lucrative business in Bantu Africa for them. Thus they engrossed themselves in it with monstrous frenzy—so much so that they roused other European powers.

Envying the obscene fortune the Portuguese were making out of the slave-trade, several European powers entered the fray like hungry hyenas on a trail of blood. Holland, Britain, Spain, and France all aggressively entered the hunt for Bantu African slaves. In 1621 the Dutch (Holland) established a slave-trading company, the Dutch West Indian Company, and had their parliament provide it with capital, soldiers, and armaments needed to hunt and capture Bantu Africans into their slavers on one hand and to defend against or attack their rivals on the other. The British followed the Dutch example and set up, by royal charter, the Royal African Company on 20th September, 1672. In no uncertain terms King Charles II gave the Royal African Company license to conquer both rival and prey, plunder, and take control of the slave-trade:

We do hereby, for us, our heirs and successors, grant and give full power and authority under the said Royal African Company of England and their successors to enter into any ship, vessel, and attack, arrest, take and seize all manner of ships, vessels, negro slaves etc... that we, our heirs, and successors shall have and may have, take and receive two thirds of all the gold mines, which shall be found, seized, possessed in the part and places aforesaid.

And with such ferocity the British went on to become the kings of the slave-trade on both land and sea. The Spanish, who had acquired huge colonies for themselves in the Americas that were in need of Bantu African slave labour to develop them, ended up relying on the British to supply them with the much needed Bantu African slaves. And to this effect, the British Monarchy and Spanish Monarchy even signed fiercely binding contracts called *Asientos* whose breaching was under pain of war. One such Asiento signed in 1701 by the British and Spanish Monarchies Read:

Contract for Blacks or Negroes [Bantu Africans] made by the King of Spain and Agreed with Her Majesty the Queen of Great Britain for Herself and such of Her Subjects as she shall appoint to be Contractors.

With license from Her Majesty, the contractors upon thee the Asiento or Agreement to import negro slaves into the Spanish West Indies [the Americas and the Caribbean], and to establish this necessary trade for the united and reciprocal benefit of their Majesties and the subjects of both crowns, and the contractors oblige themselves to import in the space of 10 years, 48 000 negroes of both sexes.

The entry of Holland, Great Britain, Spain, and France into the slave-trade had ghastly ramifications for Bantu Africans everywhere. Whereas the Portuguese had mainly perpetrated their slave raids in the Kongo Kingdom and surrounding areas, the new entrants took slave raids to the rest of Bantu Africa in a bid to capture more Bantu Africans into slavery and meet their targets as can be seen in the above *Asiento,* for instance—*"48 000 negroes of both sexes in a space of 10 years."* But Bantu Africa being vast, impassable in most places, and inhospitable to foreigners (due to the prevalence of deadly tropical diseases such as malaria), these new European slavers, despite descending on Bantu Africa in their huge, well-equipped armies, could not commit their enormities on Bantu Africans without local accomplices. Like the Portuguese before them, they enlisted some Bantu African groups to help them capture their neighbours; and many Bantu African kings and chiefs, out of their proverbial avarice, readily took to having their own people captured and sold to these European slavers as though they were selling their herds of cattle to travelling butchers.

Documenting the widespread strife European slavers brought in almost every part of Bantu Africa and the complicity of Bantu African kings and chiefs, D.E. Needham, E.K. Mashingaidze, and N. Bhebe in *From Iron Age to Independence, A History of Central Africa,* write of the plight of the Chewa people of today's Malawi, Zambia, and Mozambique under their chiefs when this plague of slave raids hit their chiefdom:

At this time there was a big demand for slaves and these were being bought from subordinate chiefs. The growing demand for slaves resulted in increased conflicts and warfare in [Undi's Chewa] the Kingdom because wars provided slaves. Larger numbers of people were being accused of witchcraft and sorcery so that they could be sold as slaves. As chief fought against chief, travel in Undi area became unsafe. The Swahili slavers also joined the Portuguese and Chikundas [Portuguese hired Bantu African slave raiders] in the slave raiding campaigns. Undi's Kingdom became more and more unstable and the prospect of final collapse drew nearer.

To all intents and purposes for Holland, Great Britain, Spain, and France to have joined Portugal in assailing Bantu Africa for slaves, the world's super powers had in effect declared to wage a protracted and devastating war on Bantu

Africa—it was like the entire might of NATO, to which incidentally all 5 of them are now leading members, invading and ravaging for hundreds of years SADC countries of Africa, which nearly constitute Bantu Africa. Apart from having almost half of Bantu Africa under their brutal occupation for so many years (in fact, most of them never ever left Bantu Africa to this day), the slave raids they orchestrated in Bantu Africa were essentially murderous and devastating battles of a long atrocious war. As some Bantu African groups tried to fight off the slavers and their hired raiders, many of them were massacred, maimed, displaced, and dispossessed.

Around the 1640s, for instance, the legendary Queen Nzinga of Bantu Africa's Ndongo and Matamba people, the Kongo Kingdom's immediate southern neighbours, skilfully rallied all their surrounding Bantu African groups—the Imbangala, Kongos, Kissama, Ovimbundu, and, indeed, the ferocious Jaga who usually hired themselves out to the Portuguese slavers—to fight off the Portuguese in their lands and protect themselves from further slave raids; despite putting up a spirited fight against the Portuguese who, in fact, found themselves fighting a war on two fronts as they were also under attack from the Dutch who wanted to drive them out of that part of Bantu Africa, they were all routed. Many of them, including their chiefs, save Queen Nzinga herself and the Manikongo who were captured and put under permanent house arrest, were butchered by the Portuguese. As writes Basil Davidson in *Old Africa Rediscovered:*

[The Portuguese and their European compatriots who came to wage slave wars in Bantu Africa] were schooled in the bitter

rivalries of Europe ... they were better armed. They were trained to ruthlessness. They wanted more than a simple monopoly of trade, ruinous though that would be ...; they wanted loot as well. African warfare, like Indian warfare, was designed to minimize casualties, not maximize them. These invaders had no such care.

For nearly 300 years, 16th – 19th century, in which the world's mightiest nations then—Portugal, Holland, Great Britain, Spain , and France—descended on Bantu Africa and waged a ruthless slave war against its hapless people, Bantu Africa lay utterly wasted. At a time when Europeans themselves were making tremendous progress in all fields of human endeavours with their political and industrial revolutions, Bantu Africa's economic, social, and political progress came to a halt: millions of its productive sons and daughters were either being wrenched into slavery or massacred for resisting; the very old and very young were left to die of famines, having been dispossessed and displaced. Those able-bodied who survived this ordeal at all were never in a sane state as to drive progress in a horribly ravaged and largely insecure place, apart from being traumatized by the horrors of helplessly seeing their brothers and sisters awfully captured or massacred, they themselves were stripped of everything, as the slave raiders also took away their livestock and many valuables. The unprecedented prosperity Europeans attained between the 16th and the 19th centuries while Bantu Africans were being ruined by the slave-trade may rightly be attributed to their own ingenuity as testified by their epoch-making scientific and technological innovations, but there can be no denying that it was fuelled by the blood and sweat of Bantu Africans. John

Hippisley (17-- – 1776), an officer of the18[th] century Great Britain's Company of Merchants Trading to Africa, formerly the chartered Royal African Company, we saw above, and who was later appointed Governor of the Cape Coast Castle, Great Britain's slave-trading fort on the Gold Coast (Ghana), eloquently admitted in one of his essays, '*On the Populousness of Africa*':

The extensive employment of our shipping in, to, and from America, the great brood of seamen that consequent there on and the daily bread of the most considerable part of our British manufacturing are owing primarily to the labour of Negroes.

The Negro trade and the natural consequences resulting from it may justly be esteemed an inexhaustible fund of wealth and power to this nation [Great Britain].

But that Europeans were making progress and revelling in increasing opulence at the expense of an entire hapless race did not sit well with some of their luminaries. The quiet but nagging matter of every man's inner counsel, the conscience, gave them no peace of mind over their blatant enormities against Bantu Africans. And towards the end of the 18th century they began to voice out their opposition to what was going on, to at least give solace to their troubled minds. In 1788 William Cowper (1731 – 1800) in his poem, '*Pity for the Poor Africans,*' subtly expressed both his disgust for the slave-trade and his people's obstinate obsession with its fruits:

I am shocked at the purchase of slaves,

And fear those who buy them and sell them are knaves;

What I hear of their hardships, their tortures, and groans,

Is almost enough to draw pity from stones.

I pity them greatly, but I must be mum,

For how could we do without sugar and rum?

Especially sugar, so needful we see;

What, give up our deserts, our coffee, and tea?

Besides if we do, the French, Dutch, and Danes

Will heartily thank us, no doubt, for our pains;

If we do not buy the poor creatures, they will;

And tortures and groans will be multiplied still.

But a year later William Cowper's namesake, William Wilberforce (1759 – 1833), totally convinced that the slave-trade was irredeemably wicked, called for its abolition in no uncertain terms. Addressing the British Parliament (House of Commons) on a Tuesday of 12th May 1789, Wilberforce, clearly speaking from his own troubled conscience, said:

I mean not to accuse anyone, but to take the shame upon myself,
in common, indeed, with the whole parliament of Great Britain,

for having suffered this horrid trade to be carried on under their authority. We are all guilty—we ought all to plead guilty and not to exculpate ourselves by throwing the blame on others; ...

As soon as ever I had arrived thus far in my investigations of the slave-trade, I confess to you sir, so enormous, so dreadful, so irremediable did its wickedness appear that my own mind was completely made up for the abolition. A trade founded in iniquity, and carried on as this was, must be abolished, let the policy be what it might—let the consequences be what they would, I am from this time determined that I would never rest till I had affected its abolition.

Expectedly, the condemnation of the slave-trade and slavery by Wilberforce and many European abolitionists, who shared and supported his views, sparked fierce arguments in Europe. In fact, the entire House of Commons unanimously heckled Wilberforce throughout his address. Primarily, the vast majorities of Europeans argued against calls for the abolition of the slave-trade and slavery with convincing economic reasons, which, indeed, saw Wilberforce's abolition bill, for instance, defeated repeatedly in about 20 years of its consideration in the British parliament. Wicked or not the slave-trade was the mainstay of not only Great Britain's economy but that of Europe as a whole and its abolition was understandably a dreadful economic nightmare.

But by far the most virulent arguments against the condemnation of the slave-trade and slavery were those insidiously spawned by Europe's eminent thinkers, who, having taken it upon themselves to be the architects of enlightened European thought, attempted to negate Bantu African humanity in order to absorb 'civilized' Europe of savagery crimes against humanity. Almost all leading Western philosophers accredited with shaping modern European thought advanced that Bantu Africans were not human enough to deserve humane treatment.

David Hume (1711 – 1776), a Scottish thinker, led this 18th century European philosophy of the denigration of Bantu Africans. He stated:

I am apt to suspect the Negroes to be naturally inferior to the whites. There scarcely ever was a civilized nation of that complexion, nor even any individual eminent either in action or speculation. No ingenious manufactures amongst them, no arts, no science.

On other hand, the most rude and barbarous of the Whites, such as the ancient Germans, the present Tartars, have still something eminent about them, in their valour, form of government, or some other particular. Such a uniform and constant difference could not happen, in so many countries ages, if nature had not made an original distinction between these breeds of men.

Accentuating Hume's philosophy of dehumanizing Bantu Africans on continental Europe was his disciple, Immanuel Kant (1724 – 1804), a German philosopher widely regarded as a central figure in modern philosophy, in fact, a leading authority in ethics or moral philosophy itself. He agreed with Hume that:

The Negroes of Africa have received from nature no intelligence that rises above the foolish. The difference between the two races [the other race being, of course, the European race] is thus a substantial one. It appears to be just as great in respect to the faculties of the mind as in colour.

Kant's compatriot and contemporary, Georg Hegel (1770 – 1831), a hugely influential German theological philosopher in his own right, in spite of disagreeing with much of Kant's philosophical ideas—so much so that he led the creation of a whole new branch of German philosophy called German idealism—collaborated with him in endorsing Hume's philosophy of denigrating Bantu Africans. Hegel conceded:

The Negro exhibits the natural man in his completely wild and untamed state. We must lay aside all thought of reverence and morality—all that we call feeling—if we would rightly comprehend him. There is nothing harmonious with humanity to be found in this type of character ....

And elsewhere in Europe, in France in particular, a French author and another European philosophy heavyweight, Voltaire (1694 – 1773), was of the same opinion with his above contemporaries. Although he was generally inclined to controversial views, which repeatedly landed him in serious trouble with the French authorities, he was in step with his contemporaries on the nature of Bantu Africans. He wrote that Bantu Africans *"were not capable of any great application or association of ideas."*

Thus in as much as Europe's eminent men of thought—
David Hume, Immanuel Kant, Georg Hegel, and Voltaire—are
fathers of modern European philosophies, they are also fathers
of the ugliest of Europe's modern philosophies: Racism against
Bantu Africans, a racism they diabolically sired and nurtured to
justify Europe's dispossession and exploitation of Bantu
Africans. Although many progressive European nations,
including theirs, largely disregarded this bastard of European
thought and went on to abolish the slave-trade and slavery in the
19th century, they all later embraced it to equally justify their
modified dispossession and exploitation of Bantu Africans in
the 19th and 20th centuries. The equally devastating European
imperialism, colonialism, and, indeed, apartheid in Bantu
Africa, which followed on the heels of the slave-trade and
slavery, was firmly grounded in the philosophy of the
denigration of Bantu Africans, aka Racism.

Just as migrations from Bantu African empires and kingdoms
did not give Bantu Africans any respite from tyranny and
dispossession, the abolition of the slave-trade in much of the
early 19th century brought them no relief. Like an AIDS victim,
who remains prone to all sorts of opportunistic killer diseases
even after a complete cure of an earlier devastating disease such
as tuberculosis, Bantu Africans lay prone to further atrocities
after Europeans had abolished the slave-trade.

And no metaphor best suits Africans at large and
comprehensively describes their predicament than AIDS; were
AIDS to mean African Immune Deficiency Syndrome, it would
still be accurate to all intents and purposes.

And again just as an HIV virus causes AIDS, Bantu African

rulers, like the AIDS virus, once more abetted further enormities on their people. Accustomed to living on the proceeds of the slave-trade, they continued raiding and plundering other Bantu African groups and, indeed, their subjects to procure slaves for rebel European slave-traders who continued the slave-trade long after it had been officially abolished by most European governments. While European governments had moved to sacrifice their multi-trillion-pound slave-trade-driven economies in pity of the Bantu Africans it ruined, they themselves had no such concerns even though, like Judas Iscariot, only got shillings over the heads of their people they sold into slavery; and so long as there was somebody willing to give them those few shillings over the heads of their people, so long they would kill and maim and plunder to capture their people into slavery.

The *Prazeros*, wealthy Portuguese merchants who bought huge tracts of lands (*prazos*) from Bantu African rulers to establish their own autonomous slave-procuring empires in Bantu Africa, ignored the abolition of the slave-trade. In fact, they used it to their advantage to emerge major European slave-traders who continued buying Bantu African slaves in Bantu Africa long after the abolition. Brazil, which, like the *Prazos*, was largely in the hands of wealthy Portuguese colonists who did not recognize Portuguese government authority over them nor that of any other European power and, therefore, simply disregarded the abolition of the slave-trade by these European governments, provided the *Prazeros* a huge market for their hauls of Bantu African slaves from their *prazos*. And because of this huge post-abolition Brazilian slave market, many Europeans in Bantu Africa other than the *Prazeros*, including those that were under the full authority of their European governments, which had abolished slave-trading, continued buying Bantu African slaves from Bantu African rulers to supply it.

In Angola where Portugal had established its colonial authority, Portuguese government officials themselves— policemen, soldiers, teachers, priests, and so forth—set up 'mini *prazos'* they called *sobabas*. *Sobaba* owners purported to offer Bantu Africans refuge from marauding *Pombeiros*, Angolan Bantu African slave raiders, but in actual fact they were also ingeniously procuring Bantu African slaves to sell to slave-trade merchants who served the Brazilian slave market. The Portuguese *sobaba* owners would, indeed, offer some Bantu Africans refuge in their *sobabas* but, ironically, they would in turn ask them to pay them for that kindness in slaves. Thus for over 50 years after the abolition of the slave-trade, that is from 1836, when Portugal officially abolished its trans-Atlantic slave-trade, to 1890, when she forcibly took over *prazos* to suppress their slave procuring and trading activities, about 3 million more Bantu Africans were shipped into slavery in Brazil via the *prazos* and *sobabas*—thanks to the complicity of Bantu African rulers and men of influence.

Matching the Portuguese, and perhaps surpassing them, in colluding with Bantu African rulers and men of influence in ravaging and decimating Bantu Africans in the 19th century were the Arabs, especially the Oman Sultanate, who wrested the Island of Zanzibar from the Portuguese in 1698 and went on to turn it into a leading Arab centre of trade in spices, ivory, and slaves off the coast of East Africa. Unlike Europeans who were all mainly trans-Atlantic slavers, the Omanians, and many Arabs and Swahilis, were Red Sea and Indian Ocean slavers. They virtually lived in a world of their own. They were largely unaffected by European developments such as the 19th century movement to abolish the slave-trade and slavery in Europe, the Americas, and the Caribbean. And even in Bantu Africa itself where they mostly ran into Europeans while in search of the same commodities—slaves and ivory—they had their won marked hunting ground: Zanj Empire, East and Central Bantu Africa. And once they procured their slaves and ivory, they again served their own markets in the Middle East, the Persian Peninsular, Madagascar, India, and so forth, which were in high demand of Bantu African slaves and ivory just like the Americas, the Caribbean, and Europe were.

And then they were not Christian like Europeans, who abolished their slave-trade evoking Christian ethos; they were Muslims whose faith, Islam, permitted slavery. Thus, with only the Portuguese to reckon with where their paths met, the Arabs callously orchestrated relentless raids for Bantu African slaves in the 19th century. And at their service to perpetrate those raids were Bantu African rulers and merchants with their armies of raiders. Whereas the Portuguese had in their service the Pombeiros, Lozi, Luvale, and Chikunda who raided the Tswana, Nkhoya, Kaonde, and Chewa, etc., the Arabs had the Bemba, Bisa, and Yao who preyed on the Lungu, Mambwe, Lomwe, and so forth. And just as the Portuguese had the *prazeros* and *sobaba* owners procuring slaves for them through their *prazos* and *sobabas*, the Arabs had powerful and wealthy Zanj merchants, who established vast slave-procuring empires in East and Central Bantu Africa.

Msiri (c. 1830 – 1891), through plundering many Bantu African groups and overthrowing their chiefs, established his *Garanganze* kingdom in present day DR Congo's Katanga area from about 1856 to 1891. From *Garanganze,* and for over a period of 30 years of his reign till he was killed by Belgian colonial forces on December 20, 1891, he had all of central Bantu Africa ransacked for slaves, which, being in that central position in Katanga, he managed to sell to both the Portuguese on the South-Western coast of Bantu Africa and the Arabs on the Eastern coast.

Similarly, Tippu Tip, whose real name was quite a marathon: Mohammed bin Jumah bin Rajab el Murjebi (1837 – 1905), established himself, through brutal conquests and slave raids, a vast empire that stretched from much of eastern DR Congo over Lake Tanganyika and Lake Victoria and up to Bagamoyo on the eastern coast of Bantu Africa. Rendering East and Central Bantu Africa, or Zanj, a land of despicable horrors, many such 19th century Bantu African slave-trade merchants—Salim bin Abdullah aka Chief Jumbe, Chief Makanjira, Chief Mponda, Mlozi, etc., all of Malawi, Chief Mirambo in Tanzania, Nyungu Yamawe in Kenya, and, indeed, the Bantu African groups they collaborated with, such as the formidable Ruga-Ruga slave raiders and the Nyamwezi of Tanzania, the Baganda and Banyoro of Uganda, the Akamba of Kenya, and the Khartoumers of Sudan, to name but the most notorious—all carved up the entire East and Central Bantu Africa into their respective slave raiding empires.

Indeed, in all Bantu Africa not a single Bantu African chief or merchant was ever spared from selling his people to the Arab and Swahili slavers or offering them up as tribute of slaves to the mighty slave-trade emperors such as Msiri and Tippu Tip in the 19th century. And to this day, 21st century, the relationship between a Bantu African chief and his subjects is that of master and slaves.

The chiefs of my own Bantu African group, the Chewa, for instance, still regard their subjects as *akapolokumene* (virtual slaves); they expect them to behave as such before them or else heavy fines in form of herds of cattle and goats and, indeed, expulsions from their villages, which formerly would have meant being disposed of into slavery, are often meted out to those who flout subservient customary conduct.

When all the factors that made for the slave-trade and slavery that doomed Bantu Africans to carnage, ruin, and anguish for nearly 300 years are taken into consideration, especially the shocking awful role Bantu African men of influence played in it all from start to finish, the occasional listless demands for reparations, say, from Europeans for their role, made by some Bantu African scholars and leaders, are a sham, to say the least.

Bantu African rulers and merchants and their bands of Bantu African slave raiders are directly responsible for over 90% of the slaves that left Congo, Sudan, Kenya, Uganda, Tanzania, Malawi, Zambia, Mozambique, South Africa, Zimbabwe, Botswana, and Angola to the Americas, the Caribbean, Europe, the Middle East, the Persian Peninsular, India and many Indian Ocean Islands and an equal amount that perished and those that were left anguished in the process.

Of all Africans, Bantu Africans should be the last to ask for reparations for the slave-trade and slavery from anybody— European or Arab. Neither do they deserve any apology from anybody—European or Arab! And attempts to have the remorse Europeans and, indeed, the whole world feel for the Holocaust to apply to even the slave-trade and slavery Bantu Africans suffered are not only misplaced but an insult to Jews. Because no Jew ever helped Europeans, or indeed, captured fellow Jews and drove them into NAZI concentration camps. Perhaps in West Africa where such calls for reparations and apologies are made vociferously and where Europeans left grim slave castles and dungeons as incontrovertible evidence of their culpability and where Samuel L. Jackson (b.1948) depicts Kunta Kinte in a film, *Roots*, as having been captured against the will of the rulers there—perhaps there Africans did not take their fellow Africans into slavery. But even there those raiders chasing Kunta and nabbing him with heavy chains are clearly black as Bantu Africans.

As though the slave raids Bantu Africans visited on each other for about 300 years were not horrible enough, some other purely Bantu African groups—not a single European or Arab among them—the Ngoni and the Ndebele, stomped out of Southern Bantu Africa, fleeing the murderous *mfecane* wars of King Shaka (1787 – 1828) of the Bantu African Zulu people, only to unleash untold mayhem themselves on all other Bantu African groups they encountered in their long march from Southern Bantu Africa to Central and Eastern Bantu Africa.

Indeed, the violent march of the Ngoni into Central and Eastern Bantu Africa can be likened to Mao Zedong (1893 – 1976) and his people's famous 1934-35 long march from Eastern China into Central and Northern China, which was undertaken for similar reasons—fleeing a murderous regime. But the similarities should end there. Because whereas Mao Zedong and his followers endeavoured and succeeded to win the support of central and northern Chinese peasants, and returned to Eastern and Southern China and chased General Chiang Kai-Shek (1887 – 1975) and his Kuomintang (the Nationalist People's Party) out of mainland China onto the Island of Taiwan, and in the process liberating many Chinese peasants who suffered the Kuomintang bloody reign, Zwangendaba (1785 – 1848), the Ngoni leader, and his people never returned to Southern Bantu Africa to drive the warlike King Shaka and his cohorts out of mainland Bantu Africa onto, say, Robben Island and free Bantu Africans from their enormities. They chose to permanently settle in the lands of their refuge in present day Tanzania, Malawi, Mozambique, and Zambia. And there instead of winning the support and love of Central and Eastern Bantu Africans, their new neighbours, they settled on inflicting such gruesome attacks on them that the slave raids they usually suffered at the hands of Bantu African slave raiders began to look like ordinary forays of local bandits recruiting new members to their gangs. The Ngoni and, indeed, the Ndebele like their parent group, the Zulu, raised regiments of thousands of young men, which the Ngoni like the Zulu called *impis* and the Ndebele called *amajaha*, specifically to butcher their neighbours—not to capture them alive and drive them into slavery, but with their sharp assegais instantly and ruthlessly kill them in combat, rustle all their livestock, and take over their women as spoils of war.

For much of the 19th century, 1820s – 1890s, the Ngoni and Ndebele and, indeed, the Zulu themselves massacred, robbed, and raped their neighbours, who in many instances, especially in Central and Eastern Bantu Africa, had already been greatly impoverished and deeply traumatized by the slave raids. And once more, like during many grim years of the European and Arab orchestrated slave raids, Bantu Africa was turned pitch black with bloodbaths, mayhem, anguish, and despair. And just as most human activities come to a halt in pitch darkness, once more in all Bantu Africa productivity stalled. Producers, Bantu Africans, and their products, crops and livestock, were lost to the *impis* and the *amajaha*. And nothing productive either ever came from the Bantu African raiding groups themselves. Year in and year out, they were sustained by bloody loot.

Apart from modifying and honing their assegais, the Zulu, Ndebele, and Ngoni like the slave-raiding Yao, Bemba, Nyamwezi, to mention but a few, hardly knew a year of decent productivity in the 19th century. And this was the pathetic Bantu Africa European missionaries, on one hand, came to redeem from a possible self-annihilation and European colonists, on another, came to further exploit towards the end of the 19th century.

3

European

Rescue and Exploitation

When the missionaries came to Africa they had the Bible and we had the land. They said 'Let us pray'. We closed our eyes. When we opened them we had the Bible and they had the land.

—Archbishop Desmond Tutu.

For a colonized people the most essential value, because the most concrete, is first and foremost land, the land which will bring them bread and, above all, dignity.

—Frantz Fanon.

Was it not enough punishment and suffering in history that we were uprooted and made helpless slaves not only in new colonial outposts but also domestically?

—Robert Mugabe.

There is no phenomenon in the entire tragic history of Bantu Africans that they have been so drilled to loath than their colonization by Europeans at the end of the 19thcentury. Their mass dispossessions and exterminations at the hands of their kings and emperors in the Age of African Empires and Kingdoms (13th – 16th century), the devastating plunder and slave raids visited on them by their 17th – 18th century migrant rulers, the ravages and bloodbaths of the *mfecane*, and the enormities of the 19th century Bantu African on Bantu African slave raids—all seem to be blotted by little more than half a century, 1890s – 1960s, of the European colonization of Bantu Africa. From then on Bantu Africans—be them academics, students, writers, revolutionaries, politicians, economists, activists of all sorts, religious leaders, diplomats, and, indeed, ordinary people begin to see the European colonization of Bantu Africa as the greatest evil to have ever befallen Bantu Africans.

But for all its demonization and for all the battering it received at the hands of Bantu African nationalists and freedom fighters, the European colonization of Bantu Africa was a lifeline of Bantu Africans. Of course, as we shall see later, Europeans, astute as ever, quickly turned this lifeline, as soon as it saved Bantu

Africans, into a leash around their necks, and no doubt the main reason for their enduring rabid strain at it. All the same, it was never conceived to further torment them the way it did. And neither was it conceived by heartless European imperialists, who turned it into a vicious leash around their necks. No, it was conceived by selfless holy men of Europe, the European Christian missionaries to Bantu Africa—the likes of Dr David Livingstone (1813 – 1873)—who, in their desperate attempts to stem the atrocities of the seemingly endless 19th century Bantu African on Bantu African slave and livestock raids, called upon their governments, with great difficult and persuasion, to adopt Bantu African territories with nothing more than *corrective colonization.*

Many European societies in the 19th century totally abhorred the slave-trade and slavery wherever they continued to be practiced throughout the world. Probably out of genuine human compassion, they felt and expressed great sympathy in many a forum and media for the African victims of the scourge. Thus they prompted their governments to wage a relentless, worldwide crusade against the entire slave-trade industry. Great Britain, for one, committed her then superior Royal Navy to fight the industry at sea. She also spent huge sums of the her taxpayers money to compensate several slave-trading nations for losses they incurred due to her anti-slavery activities and she signed numerous anti-slave trade treaties with almost every slave-trading nation or people in the world. Even with the Muslim Oman Sultanate who controlled Zanzibar and fuelled the fierce slave raiding and trading in much of East and Central Bantu Africa, Great Britain signed successive anti-slave trade treaties in 1828, 1873, and 1876.

It, therefore, caused a lot of soul-searching among European societies that despite all the might efforts and sacrifices Great Britain and other European powers made, in Bantu Africa the slave-trade and all the atrocities about it raged on with increasing ferocity: every year from the 1830s to the 1880s over 20 thousand Bantu Africans were shipped to Zanzibar en route to their slavery in the Middle East, Arabia, Madagascar, India, and so forth and, as we have already seen above, an equal number or even more were in the process left displaced, maimed, and massacred.

After their soul-searching, however, European societies came to an understanding, which to this day many who have endeavoured to help solve Bantu Africa's problems still uphold, that Bantu Africans were not necessarily victims of external forces, but they were essentially victims of themselves—external forces were only exploiting Bantu Africans' self-victimization. That discerned, many European societies set out to help solve Bantu Africans' problems by addressing themselves to their primary source, the hearts and minds of Bantu Africans. The hearts and minds of Bantu Africans had become so degenerate that they no longer felt for each other nor valued human life.

Of course, today Bantu Africans boast of a philosophy of Ubuntu or Umunthu. This is a philosophy of human life they hold superior to any way of life, especially the European way of life. The philosophy of Ubuntu regards benevolence towards others or one's community as a true mark of one's humanity in contrast to his or her basic selfish, animal nature. And the philosophy cites and exalts the Bantu African way of life as its prototype (hence the term Ubuntu, derived from Bantu), for it is held to perfectly exemplify this benevolence towards others in its supposed understanding that one exists in so far as his community exists: "I am because we are," goes the supposed maxim of the African way of life. This is then sharply contrasted with what is held as the European way of life which presupposes that one exists in so far as he thinks, as expressed in the supposed European maxim of life: "*Cogito Ergo Sum*"*(I* am because I think).

Yes, in their exaltation of the philosophy of Ubuntu Bantu

African thinkers hold this supposed egoistic European way of life contemptible and responsible for the rampant individualism in European societies. But, in actual fact, no any other people than Bantu Africans themselves have exhibited, through the centuries since the Age of African Empires and Kingdoms and all the way up to the coming of European missionaries and colonialists in the 19th century, a staggering lack of regard for one another. A chief, as we have already seen, would have his own people violently captured and sold into slavery just as a neighbour would callously raid his neighbourhood for slaves and livestock, and sometimes butcher his neighbour, and take over his wives to be added to those he already had.

The philosophy of Ubuntu, never mind its wonderful appeal nor the African greats, who espouse it, is clearly of dubious origins, as far as the history of Bantu Africans' way of life is concerned. Very probably it could have arisen together with Bantu African nationalistic sentiments in the 20th century, and was obviously generated by European educated Bantu Africans who wanted to oppose Europeans in thought and deed.

Nevertheless, Europeans in the 19th century believed that rehabilitating the degenerate hearts of Bantu Africans with Christianity and enlightening their ignorant minds with education and then providing them with better alternative occupations to their raiding way of life, such as farming, carpentry, bricklaying, and trading in mineral and wildlife resources, were ultimate acts in any of their redemption—be it in body or in soul. They established and sponsored Christian missionary societies, such as the London Missionary Society, they thought could better undertake these acts in Bantu Africa. And Many European individuals and groups, perhaps bidding for sainthood, which wasn't uncommon nor zany among many Christian communities then, or practically sensing in it all a 'holy' opportunity to make their own fortune out of Bantu

Africa, as many had done before them or, indeed, out of sheer desire for philanthropic work and exploration, as was the case with Dr David Livingstone, volunteered to become Christian missionaries to Bantu Africa.

But once in Bantu Africa many of them found their missions literally impossible, frustrating and extremely costly. As could have been expected, most Bantu African rulers who lived on raiding rejected the missionaries and their missions outright. They even refused them residence anywhere near their territories or in the neighbouring territories of other Bantu African groups they considered their raiding grounds. And in such hostile circumstances a lot of missionary zeal cost many missionaries their lives. And the proverbial Bantu African in hospitable environment, which is infested with killer tropical diseases such as malaria, also took its toll on their lives. And those who survived this harsh reception at all ended up finding their crosses far too big to bear alone. When they succeeded against all odds to establish their missionary outposts—churches, schools, workshops, et cetera, they repeatedly saw them ransacked and burnt down completely by Bantu African raiders who still came to raid their very converts, students, asylum seekers, and so forth into the slave-trade.

As a result, many European missionaries deeply depressed and frustrated, found themselves sailing back to Europe to report the horrors they had encountered and to advise their sponsors and, indeed, their governments what they thought would help their missions in Bantu Africa.

Dr David Livingstone, for one, returned to Great Britain after his first mission to Bantu Africa and, in 1856, embarked on publishing books, conducting lectures at universities, and giving speeches around Great Britain, narrating the atrocities he had encountered in Bantu Africa but at the same time recounting the amazing discoveries he had made, the awesome natural and wild life resources Bantu Africa possessed, and the enormous potential for lucrative commerce he thought Bantu Africa thus offered other than the vile slave-trade. He passionately implored businessmen to accompany missionaries to Bantu Africa to go and establish alongside their missionary establishments alternative business ventures with Bantu African rulers such as mining, wild life hunting, and production and sale of industrial crops like cotton, coffee, tea, tobacco, etc., to wean them from the slave-trade. He also appealed to the British government to seriously consider sending some military forces to Bantu Africa to at least protect those missionary and business establishments.

In the light of the enduring myth of the European Scramble for Africa, one would think it unlikely or outright false that the missionaries ever needed to implore their governments and businessmen to come to Bantu Africa. The phrase European Scramble for Africa connotes Europeans ravenously swooping down on Bantu Africa or Africa at large in droves and carving it up among themselves without any urging.

Well, European missionaries not only pleaded with their governments and business compatriots to establish their presence in Bantu Africa but, contrary to the connotation of a scramble, they also had their requests turned down in much of the 19th century. Despite the pity they felt for ravaged, poor Bantu Africans, many European societies, let alone their governments, were not keen to commit to Bantu Africa anything more than their odd missionary compatriots and their Bibles. The missionaries' call for military forces to sail to Bantu Africa and get based in its interior to protect European business establishments and their missions bordered on European governments practically establishing protectorates and colonies there, a thing they considered undesirable until the 20th century.

Despite the Dutch, English, and Portuguese having already

settled in a few choice territories in Southern Bantu Africa, for most Europeans much of Bantu Africa was simply unsuitable for European settlement. The tropical, killer diseases which Dr Livingstone and a few of his colleagues had then just survived only to tell how they but wiped out most of their unfortunate colleagues and their entire families[3], stories of horrible savagery and bloody strife in Bantu Africa, the scotching tropical heat, the complete wilderness of Bantu Africa with absolutely no infrastructure to support a good life, all made Bantu Africa repulsive.

And even when they finally conceded towards the end of the 19th century, it was with such reluctance that they either sent only a few military personnel, which they asked the missionaries themselves to host at their mission stations or asked Bantu African-based European entrepreneurs, such as Cecil Rhodes (1853 – 1902), to hire and provide some military security to missionary establishments.

And this situation hardly improved the security of many missionary establishments nor stemmed the cattle and slave raids that still affected their converts and Bantu Africans at large. Stubborn Bantu African slave and cattle raiders, who by this time also wielded guns, kept running over less protected mission stations.

On the other hand, exceptional adequately protected mission stations literally became salvation camps for thousands and thousands of Bantu Africans who were constantly persecuted by slave raiders. One such mission in today's Northern Province of Zambia has retained the local name, '*Chilubula*,' it earned for providing that relief. '*Chilubula*,' literally means a place of rescue. Chilubula Mission was given its name by Bantu Africans who took

---

[3]Dr David Livingstone himself fell ill on his third and last mission to Bantu Africa and died of malaria in what is today Zambia.

refuge at it from Bemba and Swahili slave raiders and traders. This mission was founded in the mid-1890s by Fr. Joseph DuPont (1850 – 1930), a militant French Catholic missionary of the Society of Missionaries of Africa (aka White Fathers) and a veteran of the Franco-Prussian war. Using his military experience much more than his priestly virtues, and thereby earning himself a nickname of 'Moto Moto' (the fiery one) from the natives, Fr. DuPont succeeded to keep the Bemba and Swahili slave raiders at bay until, with the help of Cecil Rhodes' British South African Company (BSA Company) military forces he later enlisted, despite being French himself, he had them totally defeated in 1898 to the overwhelming relief of many Bantu Africans there.

And it was for this sort of salvation, physical rescue from ruthless slave raiders as opposed to spiritual salvation, that many Bantu Africans joined the missionaries in calling on Europeans to out right make their territories European protectorates or colonies. For instance, taking advantage of Cecil Rhodes' BSA Company forces Fr. DuPont had engaged, Chief Chiwara of the Senga people, who repeatedly suffered Bemba and Swahili slave raids, asked Robert '*Bobo*' Young, a military officer who was in-charge of the BSA Company forces, to extend their control to his troubled area. And Bobo Young and the BSA Company forces obliged. And when the Bemba and the Swahili next attacked his chiefdom, not knowing that it was now under the protection of the BSA Company forces, they met their Waterloo. The BSA Company forces routed the Bemba and Swahili slave raiders, chased those who fled all the way to their fortified villages or bomas, destroyed their bomas *completely*, and freed hundreds of slaves they had been holding from Chief Chiwara's Senga people and others. And from then on Chief Chiwara's territory, those of other surrounding Bantu African groups, and, indeed, the once greatly feared Bemba territories themselves all fell under British control as part of what became known as the British North Eastern Rhodesia, albeit, and as the name suggests, under the auspices of Cecil Rhodes' BSA Company who the British government had chartered, after the 1884-85 presumed scramble for Africa, to administer the territories she had 'scrambled for' in Bantu Africa.

Similarly, in what is today's Western and North Western Zambia, Litunga(King) Lubosi Lewanika (1842 – 1916) of the Lozi in fear of the Ndebele raids asked his resident missionary, Francois Collard(1858 – 1905), in 1885 to write to Queen Victoria (1819 – 1901) of Great Britain requesting her and the British government to colonize his Kingdom. But Cecil Rhodes and his BSA Company again, after disposing of a series of seedy concessions the not-so-straightforward Litunga Lewanika entered into with several European speculators while waiting for Queen Victoria's response, as we shall see later, ended up taking control of the territory in 1887 and had it called North-Western Rhodesia.

And Cecil Rhodes and the BSA Company later, in 1911, merged North Eastern Rhodesia and North Western Rhodesia into a British protectorate of Northern Rhodesia, which is present-day Zambia.

But, by and large, nothing short of maximum use of military force and bringing Bantu Africa under total European control or colonization would have stopped the catastrophic raiding way of life of most prominent Bantu African groups. Certainly, not the 1884-85 paper Scramble for Africa alone, which was conjured up in the comfort of the German Chancellor's Berlin conference room in Europe, and which when matched with the supposed scramblers' real influence in Bantu Africa, it may well have been as good as a scramble for Mars: save for Cecil Rhodes and his BSA Company, Great Britain had no real influence in much of its presumed territories in Southern Bantu Africa; and King Leopold II (1835 – 1909) of Belgium, who personally 'scrambled' what is now the DR Congo (which is almost twice the size of Europe itself) for a mere song (he convinced his fellow *'scramblers'* that if they let him have it all, he would allow all of them, their governments, and people to conduct their affairs in it, and hence the name Congo Free State), did not have a single Belgian national in it for many years but a his friend and agent, Henry Morton Stanley (1841 – 1904), the British American explorer and journalist who was working for the New York Times and who in 1871famously met Dr Livingstone at Ujiji, in present-day Tanzania, with the memorable salutation, *"Dr Livingstone, I presume?"*

Neither did European missionary and business establishments backed by minimal European security, as was espoused by most missionaries, come anywhere near their intended noble goal of giving Bantu Africans a new lease of life, a happier peaceful life; when pitted against the relentless slave and cattle raiders of Bantu Africa, they fared no better than a few buckets of water and a couple of green branches desperately thrown at a raging Savannah bush fire to put it out.

And nowhere was the need for total *corrective* colonization of Bantu Africa so pronounced, nowhere was the inefficacy of a theoretical scramble for Africa and the inadequacy of isolated secure European missionary and business establishments so brutally exposed, than in what is today Zimbabwe.

When Great Britain virtually left its territories in the hands of Cecil Rhodes after the 1884-85 Berlin partitioning of Africa, Rhodes faced a mammoth challenge of populating the territories with the unwilling British people. So he ended up issuing enticing adverts to the British public in Great Britain and nearby South Africa that he needed all kinds of settlers—builders, carpenters, farmers, traders, blacksmiths, teachers, doctors, nurses, security men, et cetera—to come and settle in his territories for a reward of 3 000 acres of land each. And free 3 000 acres of land to each settler can as well show how much it took to bring the unwilling

Europeans to come and settle in Bantu Africa. Still, only about 200 Europeans responded positively, and mainly from South Africa.

This group, which became known as the Pioneers, made a grand entry into Southern Rhodesia (Zimbabwe) from South Africa in 1890 escorted by 400 mounted men and 1000 foot soldiers Cecil Rhodes hired from Chief Khama of the Bantu African Ngwato people of Botswana. And once in Rhodesia, the pioneers built their settlement in Eastern Rhodesia or Mashonaland, the land of the Bantu African Shona people who constantly fell victim to the raids of their Bantu African Ndebele neighbours of Western Rhodesia or Matabeleland, the land of the Ndebele. The Pioneers named their main settlement Fort Salisbury (which today is Harare) in honour of the British Conservative Prime Minister, Lord Salisbury aka Robert Arthur Talbot Gascoigne-Cecil (1830 – 1903) whose government gifted Cecil Rhodes these British territories. Some Pioneers immediately took to farming and cattle raring on their 3 000acres of lands each received even in places like the Masvingo districts of Mashonaland. Although all these European settlements were well clear of the territories of the militant Ndebele, they, the Ndebele, took issue with them. D.E. Needham, E.K. Mashingaidze, and N. Bhebe in their book, *From Iron Age to Independence, A History of Central Africa*, remark that: *"As far as the Ndebele were concerned, white settlers' occupation of Eastern Zimbabwe had made no difference to the fact that it was their traditional raiding ground."*

So three years after the Pioneers had settled down to a promising agricultural, industrial, and commercial life, cultivating their 3 000-acre-lands, raising livestock, processing their produce, and exporting to South Africa, which had a large European population and hence a substantial market, Lobengula (1845 - 1894), the then Ndebele King, sent 3 000 of his amajaha, young Ndebele warriors, under the command of an equally young commander, Mgandani, to ransack the Masvingo area of Eastern Rhodesia. History has it that King Lobengula actually instructed Mgandani to only have the amajaha attack their fellow Bantu Africans, the Shona, and never hurt any European or touch European property in the area. But whatever the case, in the heat of the raid Mgandani and this 3 000-strong amajaha force could not tell Shona herds of cattle from those of Europeans in that both were herded by Shona herdsmen either as European employees or as herders of their own cattle. Neither could Mgandani and the amajaha realize that an attack on the Shona who were now European employees was tantamount to hurting Europeans themselves and touching their property. So they indiscriminately rustled both Shona and European herds of cattle, killed and maimed many Shonas without regard or possibly knowing whether they were European employees or not, and similarly took as spoils of war hundreds of Shona women and girls who were either working for Europeans or not and in the process they savagely disrupted European farming, industrial, commercial, and social activities.

And that brutally it finally dawned on the Europeans, not only the shell-shocked Pioneers and Cecil Rhodes, but also the reluctant British government and Queen Victoria that total corrective colonization of all of Bantu Africa was imperative. All of them, united by the rude reality, now committed themselves to rooting out root and branch the raiding way of life in Bantu Africa, beginning with a decisive response to King Lobengula's amajaha raids to set the standard. The Queen and the British government gave Cecil Rhodes all their blessings and support to raise a formidable settler army to conquer the Ndebele and bring all of Southern Rhodesia under total British control.

Using the same enticement, in fact, more than double, as he used to woo the Pioneers into Southern Rhodesia, Cecil Rhodes, now acting through Dr Leander Starr Jameson(1853 – 1917), who was then the commissioner of Southern Rhodesia, as he himself was now the Prime Minister of South Africa's Cape Colony, raised a volunteer army of 1 100 Europeans. He promised each one of them over 6 000 acres of land in their chosen part of Matabeleland, plus a fair share of King Lobengula's and, indeed, the Ndebele's cattle, and, to crown it all, 20 gold claims. And to this hugely motivated 1 100 volunteer force he added 2 000 Tswana foot soldiers he again hired from Chief Khama and 400 Shona and Cape Colony Bantu African auxiliary fighters, who were mostly employees of European settlers. Altogether he enlisted 3 500 fighters to not only take on the 3 000 amajaha who had run over the Masvingo area but the entire Ndebele Kingdom which had a standing army of about 18 000 fighters, who were no less formidable than their Zulu counterparts and forbearers in South Africa who had already dealt the British an unforgettable humiliating defeat in 1878 at Isandlwana. After all Mzilikazi, their first King and King Lobengula's father, was the Zulu Kingdom's and King Shaka's foremost general before he broke away to establish this kingdom on similar militaristic lines. Clearly Cecil Rhodes' forces were vastly outnumbered; but the most modern guns then (the Maxim and 7-pounder machine guns that his BSA Company fortune provided), their fast movement on about 8 000 horses, and hundreds of wagons of supplies compensated for the deficiency in troops.

On 1 November 1893 the Dr Leander Starr Jameson-led forces launched their offensive against the Ndebele. As expected the Ndebele put up ferocious fights in several battles of this war. But still they fell in their thousands to the Maxims and 7-pounders.

Sensing a comprehensive defeat, King Lobengula fled Matabeleland never to return and leaving his people at the mercy of Dr Jameson's forces. And on 4 November 1893 Dr Jameson's forces raised the Union Jack in burning Bulawayo (the capital of Matabeleland), signalling the complete takeover of all of Matabeleland by the British.

After the war, Cecil Rhodes, with the approval of Queen Victoria and the British government, honoured his promises to the victorious European fighters. He let each one of them take up his chosen 6 000plus acre portion of Matabeleland. The hugely decimated leaderless Ndebele, who were found on such chosen lands, were all driven into dry infertile Shangani and Gwaaii reserves where, ironically, considering that these were infertile lands and the Ndebele had always been raiders and never farmers, they were given seeds to plant. And again in some kind of poetic justice, considering that King Lobengula had about 250 000 herds of cattle he acquired through his amajaha's periodic raids of other Bantu African groups, Cecil Rhodes equally had King Lobengula's and many Ndebele herds of cattle distributed among his victorious fighters and the rest he took for himself as royal herds. Satirically, Cecil Rhodes claimed that through his BSA Company that had assumed total control of Matabeleland, he had succeeded King Lobengula as the new king of the Ndebele!

From then on, with the standard well set in Matabeleland, the British earnestly took up the role of the scourge of all pro-slavery and raiding societies in all British Bantu Africa. Invigorated with the crushing of the formidable Ndebele raiders, the British now became convinced that any tyrannical society around them—be it Bantu African, Arab, or European—could be dealt with similarly and redeem British Bantu Africa for egalitarian British imperialism.

Thus, though it came as a surprise, and seemed unwarranted to many, that, immediately after crushing the Ndebele, Cecil Rhodes' army on 29December 1895 took on Paul Kruger's Transvaal Boer republic just south of Matabeleland in South Africa, Kruger's Boer republic, though European and officially recognized as an independent republic by Great Britain herself, perfectly fitted the description of the enemy of egalitarian British imperialism. Not only did it dispossess and oppress poor Bantu Africans it enslaved, but also other less privileged peoples like poor British settlers it called Uitlanders (foreigners) and barred from social, political, and economic participation in the Transvaal Republic. Like the Ndebele, the Boers constantly raided neighbouring Bantu African groups for land, cattle, and even slaves. In fact, the very establishment of separatist Boer republics such as the Transvaal farther North in the interior of Southern Bantu Africa in the 1840s were as a result of the Boers or the Dutch rejecting and fleeing from British anti-slavery laws and activities in the Cape, their first settlement in Bantu Africa. When in 1806 the British took over control of the Cape to prevent it falling in the hands of Napoleonic forces which had taken control of the Netherlands, the European homeland of the Dutch, they began to pass and implement egalitarian and anti-slavery laws which many of the Dutch in the Cape bitterly resented. According to the Wikipedia:

In 1828 the British authorities [in the Cape Colony] passed legislation guaranteeing equal treatment under the law for all regardless of race.... And in 1834, the government abolished slavery altogether. The Boers opposed [these] changes, as they believed they needed enslaved labour to make their farms work.

Thus in 1835 vast groups of Boers, resentful of the British egalitarian and anti-slavery administration, embarked on historic mass emigrations, the Great Trek, out of the Cape and into the interior of Southern Bantu Africa to go and establish their own pro-slavery republics—the Transvaal, the Orange Free State,

Natalia, and many smaller ones—far away from the British-controlled Cape Colony.

And when in 1886 huge gold deposits were discovered in the Transvaal and British settlers equally trekked in to partake in the colossal fortune of nature, the Boers became possessive and xenophobic—calling the incoming British Uitlanders. And this, like the final straw that broke the camel's back, prompted Cecil Rhodes to intervene with his army in 1896.

But unlike the Pioneers in Rhodesia, who rallied to Cecil Rhodes' battle cry against the Ndebele, the Uitlanders, the Transvaal version of the Pioneers, tremendously let him down. Perhaps because they were not clearly promised thousands of acres of land each in the Transvaal and stakes in its colossal gold deposits as were the Pioneers about Matabeleland, the Uitlanders, who, in fact, outnumbered the Transvaal Boers or Burghers, as they fondly called themselves, in a ratio of 2:1, did not rise to the occasion and support the Jameson Raid, as this particular Rhodes and British military operation became known after its commander (the same Dr Leander Starr Jameson who led the British volunteer army to victory over the Ndebele). And Paul Kruger's Boer Commandoes, who were but far much better armed than the Ndebele, made short work of the isolated 600 or so British Jameson raiders. Many of them were killed in 4 days of the raid— 29 December 1895 to 2 January 1896. Dr Jameson himself and other senior officers, including Cecil Rhodes' older brother, Col. Frank Rhodes, were captured and arrested by Kruger's commandoes. And following diplomatic negotiations that cost Great Britain huge sums of money in compensation to Paul Kruger's government, they were extradited to Great Britain where they were sentenced to death for high treason. Later their sentences were commuted to 15-year jail terms, but even so they were all eventually pardoned with stiff fines of £2 000 each which Cecil

Rhodes paid for them out of his BSA Company fortune. And Cecil Rhodes himself, the mastermind and sponsor of the debacle, did not go scot free. He was made to personally pay Kruger's government £1million compensation. Then the British government, desperate to save its face not only in South Africa but worldwide by attempting to be seen as totally opposed to the Jameson Raid, forced him to resign his Cape Colony premiership.

Indeed, all things considered, the British, and not only Cecil Rhodes and his army, had suffered another humiliating defeat at the hands of the Boers as they had in 1880 in the First Anglo-Boer war. But as the illustrious South African statesman, Jan C. Smuts (1870 – 1950), put it in 1906, the Jameson Raid was merely a declaration of a real epoch-making Anglo-Boer war of 4 years later over the same grievances—mistreatment of Bantu Africans and seclusion of British settlers from economic and political affairs in the Boer republics. In other words like at Isandlwana, the Jameson Raid was a battle the British truly lost, a setback they truly suffered, but only in the wider war for their corrective colonization of Bantu Africa; a war they won decisively, be it in South Africa or Bantu Africa at large.

And whereas their victory in South Africa can better be seen as winning a tortuous marathon—having suffered a terrible setback at Isandlwana before recording a series of triumphs in the Anglo-Zulu wars of1879 – 1896, and humiliating defeats in the First Anglo-Boer War of 1880-81 and in the Jameson Raid in 1896 before a landmark victory in the Second Anglo-Boer War of 1899 – 1902—in much of Bantu Africa the battles or wars were fought and won in record dash times.

In what is probably still the world record holder for the shortest war in history, 38 minutes of war which claimed about 500 lives, the British on the Island of Zanzibar, on 27 August 1896, defeated the well-armed Arabs who had ruled Zanzibar since 1868 and fuelled the most devastating slave raids in East and Central Bantu Africa for 200 years. And then we have already seen how the agents of these Arabs in East and Central Bantu Africa itself, the slave raiding Bembas and Swahilis, were routed by the British in a matter of days in 1898. And 1898 also saw the British forces overcome the stubborn Ngoni cattle raiders in Zambia and the notorious Yao slave raiders in Malawi who, at least, can be said to have almost out-sprinted the British and left them panting for breath and badly blistered. They inflicted painful loss of gallant military personnel on the British, the charismatic Captain Cecil Maguire, among them, was killed in a hail of bullets on Lake Nyasa; (Malawi)[4]. But, nonetheless, they were peeped at the finishing line thanks to British timely reinforcements with the Maxim guns, 7-pounders, 9-pounders, gunboats, a German steamer (the Hermann von Wissman lent to them by the German Anti-Slavery Society who were operating in neighbouring German East Africa, mainland Tanzania), and a contingent of 200 British Sikh troops from India.

It would seem as though by the close of the 19th century the British had simply become trigger-happy. They marked the end of this century and the beginning of the 20th century with over 500 000 British soldiers fiercely blazing their guns in the 1899 – 1902 Anglo-Boer war and 342 000 of that 500 000 British fighters were explicitly shipped from Great Britain to South Africa for that purpose, which, in fact, prompted Paul Kruger (1825 – 1904) to declare war on the British. But by 1900, the British had tried everything—treaties, persuasion, diplomacy, evangelization, bribery, deceit, threats, and so forth—to establish egalitarian British imperialism in Bantu Africa to no avail. We have seen how provocative the Ndebele were and how recalcitrant the Boers were.

---

[4]See 'Fighting the Slavers' in *Zambezi Sun rise* by W.D. Gale, Timmins, Chapter 5, pp. 111 – 125.

And about the Yao before they were defeated militarily by the British, D.E. Needham, E.K. Mashingaidze, and N. Bhebe in their book *From Iron Age to Independence, A History of Central Africa,* say: "*Not only did the Yao continue their slave trade activities, they also refused to submit to the British commissioner's authority.*" And the British commissioner in question is no other than the illustrious British explorer and colonial administrator who secured much of Central and Eastern Bantu Africa for Great Britain, Harry H. Johnson (1858 – 1927). And no one better and comprehensively accounted for the British resort to maximum force than Harry Johnson himself. In his November 1891 report to the British Foreign Office he noted:

I feel bound to make our Protectorate in Nyasaland [Malawi] a reality to the unfortunate mass of the people who are robbed, raided, and carried into captivity to satisfy the greed and lust of bloodshed prevailing among a few chiefs of the Yao race which is being unceasingly incited to engage in internecine war or slave raiding forays by the Arab and Swahili slave traders who travel between Nyasaland and the German and Portuguese littoral.

Wherever it is possible by peaceable means to induce a chief to renounce the slave trade I have done so, and a considerable number of the lesser potentates have been brought to agree to give up adjusting their internecine quarrels by resort to arms, to cease selling their subjects into slavery and to close their territories to the passage of slave caravans. Their agreement, however, was in most cases a sullen one and their eyes were turned to the nearest big chief to see how he was dealt with. If he also accepted the gospel of peace and goodwill towards men they were ready enough to co-operate; but if the powerful potentate—the champion man of war of the district—held aloof and preserved a watchful or menacing attitude towards the Administration by ignoring or rejecting our proposals for a friendly understanding, then the little chiefs began to relax in their good behaviour and once more to capture and sell their neighbours' subjects or to allow the coast caravans with their troops of slaves bound for Kilwa, Ibo, or Quilimane to pass through.

Consequently I soon realised that certain notabilities in Nyasaland would have to be compelled to give up the slave trade before our Protectorate could become a reality.

And the same was true for the cattle raiding Ngonis. They impudently refused to give up their cattle raiding activities in both Malawi and Zambia, just like their Ndebele cousins in Zimbabwe. Indeed, until the Ngoni were defeated militarily by the British on 19-20 January 1898, they not only raided and massacred their neighbours with impunity but also insulted and harassed the British authorities at will. Nsingo, a young militant M'pezeni (Ngoni Chief), made himself popular among his people by brazenly disregarding the British and repeatedly harassing them with his impis. To this day his and, indeed, the Ngoni people's intransigence, like that of the Ndebele and the Yao, has been laundered through Bantu African nationalism as early resistance to colonial rule. Nsingo, like Lobengula, rank even with all other Bantu African nationalists as nationalistic cult figures. And the British who defeated them and brought to an end their destructive raiding way of life are themselves often seen as villains, the enemy.

But surely there was absolutely nothing nationalistic about the Ngoni's or Ndebele's or, indeed, Yao's resistance to the British colonization of their territories in the 19th century. It had nothing to do with Bantu Africans' patriotic feelings. Like their resistance to missionary establishments and activities, it was all about protecting their pillaging rights and spaces just as drug lords and their gangs fiercely protect their drug-trafficking rights and territories. And Harry Johnson again in a letter to Lord Salisbury of 24 January 1896 made this very clear: *"Those enemies whom we have conquered, like all with whom we have fought since our assumption of the Protectorate, were not natives of the country fighting for their independence but aliens of Arab, Yao, or Zulu [origin] who were contesting with us for the supremacy over the natives of Nyasaland."*

And, indeed, when, for instance, the British eventually captured the unruly Nsingo, they categorically charged and executed him for "murder and raiding" and not subversion or treason for which they arrested and jailed Jomo Kenyatta (1889 – 1978), Kenneth Kaunda (b. 1924), Robert Mugabe (b. 1924), Nelson Mandela (1918 – 2013) and many genuine Bantu African nationalists. And genuine Bantu African nationalism which sired Nelson Mandela, Robert Mugabe, Kenneth Kaunda, Jomo Kenyatta, and many others, was only made possible by the European colonization of Bantu Africa itself. Never mind the irony, but it was only in the perversion of corrective colonization, only when corrective colonization horribly failed Bantu Africans, only when egalitarian imperialism turned out so vile and racist in practice, that Bantu Africans rediscovered themselves as one same people worthy of self-determination.

Once in control of Bantu Africa, European colonial authorities could not treat Bantu Africans any better than their own tyrannical emperors nor any better than their own slave and cattle raiding migrant chiefs, nor any better than the Boers and the Arabs whose villainy they, Europeans, especially the British, bitterly fought. Despite coming to Bantu Africa professing Christianity, civilization, and egalitarianism which obliged them to treat fellow

human beings with love, dignity, and equality, and for all the lives
they lost in that cause, the lives of Christian missionaries and their
families who perished at the hands of hostile Bantu African rulers
and due to tropical killer diseases and those of soldiers who fought
and perished trying to save Bantu Africans from the enormities of
slavery and plunder, and for all the resources, passion, and time
(almost a century of advocating and fighting for the freedom of
Bantu Africans from slavery), they ended up inflicting grievous
colonial injustices on Bantu Africans . To this day Bantu Africans
are in pain, anguish, and poverty. Indeed, such is the pain, anguish,
and suffering European colonial authorities caused Bantu Africans
that the historical fact that their colonization of Bantu Africa was
actually a lifeline for Bantu Africans has not only been expunged
from the memories of Bantu Africans but is now anathema to
them. Lingering in their minds are traumas of it being used
viciously by colonial authorities as a leash of terrible oppression.

The German Chancellor, Otto von Bismarck (1815 – 1885),
was the high priest of the 1884-85 partitioning of Africa which
sanctioned the European colonization of Bantu Africa. Both as
convener of the conference, which took place right in his Berlin
residence, and as a world statesman, it was he, Chancellor Otto von
Bismarck, who prevailed upon his guests and European
counterparts to commit themselves to the protection of the lives
and wellbeing of Bantu Africans they were all endeavouring to
colonize. But what his own people ended up doing in, say, German
South West Africa (Namibia), their first colony in Bantu Africa,
had all the hallmarks of a holocaust. And many have called what
the Germans did here in Namibia a blueprint to the Holocaust they
later visited on the Jews. The modus operandi of the enormities
German colonial authorities inflicted on Bantu Africans in
Namibia is chillingly similar to that of the Holocaust.

Wooed by the prospect of establishing lucrative diamond and

copper mining industries supported by an equally robust agricultural industry, 2 595 Germans went to settle in Namibia by 1902. But since the colonial policy of Germany was for colonial settlers, and not the German government, to fund their colonial endeavours, German colonial settlers elected to systematically dispossess Bantu Africans in Namibia of their lands, property, resources, and livestock as a cheaper means of making their economic headway. They crafted and imposed property ownership laws on the Bantu Africans of Namibia which in effect stripped them of their rights to the lands, resources, property, and livestock they had always held. And the land expropriation that resulted from this gifted each German settler in Namibia an average of about 3 300 acres of free land.

The Bantu African Herero people of Namibia who were then the largest Bantu African group in Namibia and the most affected by this flagrant dispossession revolted against German colonial settlers in January 1904. They attacked and killed about 150 German settlers in remote rural farms of Namibia. And the exterminating German demon swiftly descended on Namibia. The German colonial authorities ordered a complete extermination of all the Herero in Namibia by all means possible. General Lothar von Trotha (1848 – 1920), the commander of over 10 000 heavily armed German troops in Namibia, ordered for any adult Herero male to be shot on sight, all Herero water sources to be guarded by German troops, and those they couldn't guard, poisoned. And on 2 October 1904, he issued an extermination order to the Herero which read:

I, the Great General of the German troops, send this letter to the Herero people. Hereros must leave the land. If the people do not want this, then I will force them to do so with the long guns. Any Herero found within the Germany borders with or without a gun, with or without cattle, will be shot. I shall no longer receive any women and children. I'll drive them back to their people, or I will shoot them. This is my decision for the Herero.

And General Trotha haughtily signed this extermination order.

What followed was an execution of his orders to the letter by his forces. Many Hereros were massacred, their water holes were poisoned, their women and children were captured and sent to extermination camps in Windhoek, Shakopmund, and Shark Island or to concentration camps at Ludertiz, Okahandja, and Omaruru where they were used as slave labourers for German settlers or as sex slaves for German troops. Those who managed to flee from the Germans were chased all the way into the waterless Omaheke region of the Kalahari Desert where they again eventually died of thirsty.

An entire population of about 80 000 Hereros was nearly wiped out by General Trotha's 10 000-strong German troops. And the official German military report boasted of this their ruthlessness:

This bold enterprise shows up in the most brilliant light the ruthless energy of the German command in pursuing their beaten enemy. No pains, no sacrifices were spared in eliminating the last remnants of enemy resistance. Like a wounded beast the enemy was tracked from water-hole to the next, until finally he became the victim of his own environment. The arid Omaheke was to complete what the German army had begun: the extermination of the Herero.

As though unmindful of the fate of the Herero who were by far the largest Bantu African group in Namibia and who had now practically disappeared, the Nama, another Bantu African group of Namibia who numbered about 20 000 in total, also revolted against the Germans in 1905 over the same grievances of being dispossessed of their lands, livestock, and resources. And they equally met a similar fate as the Herero. They were ruthlessly massacred; and those who survived, captured and thrown into concentration and extermination camps. And General Trotha again had the audacity to pronounce the Nama's fate in another extermination order specifically addressed to them but with sadistic references to what had happened to the Herero. On 22 April 1905 he wrote to the Nama:

The Nama who chooses not to surrender and lets himself be seen in the German area will be shot, until all are exterminated. Those who, at the start of the rebellion, committed murder against whites or have commanded that whites be murdered have by law, forfeited their lives. As for the few not defeated, it will fare with them as it fared with the Herero, who in their blindness also believed that they could make successful war against the powerful German Emperor and the great German people. I ask you, where are the Herero today?

Clearly, no Herero nor Nama nor any other Bantu African people would see a lifeline in such predetermined and self-attested colonial holocausts.

But of particular interest here is what came of the much promising British corrective colonisation of Bantu Africa. While the German colonisation of Bantu Africa we have just seen was undoubtedly poisoned with disdain and malice from inception; and while almost no improvement in the welfare of Bantu Africans was expected in Portuguese Bantu African colonies, as after the 1836 Portuguese abolition of slave trading from its territories the Prazeros and Portuguese colonial authorities simply subjected the Bantu African slaves they could not export and all other Bantu Africans under their authority to Chibalo (forced labour and forced cultivation of European commercial crops such as cotton, coffee, sugar canes, and palm trees right in Bantu Africa), British colonies, on the other hand, were billed to be oases of liberty for Bantu Africans.

But what in British colonies and protectorates began as retribution for intransigent Bantu African raiding groups such as the Ndebele, Ngoni, and Zulu, quickly became the bane of all Bantu Africans under British colonial authorities. The land and livestock dispossessions, the displacements into infertile, tsetse-infested, dry lands, the anguish of being reduced to squatters in one's own ancestral land, and the pain of offering free labour to foreigners to placate them—all of which the Ndebele suffered, did not spare the Shona or any other Bantu African group who fell under British colonial control.

Indeed, British settlers may have come as liberators of, say, the Shona who were constantly preyed upon by their raiding neighbours, the Ndebele, but the British themselves showed no remorse in disinheriting them of their homeland, Mashonaland. In 1889 Cecil Rhodes and his BSA Company signed a bogus land and mining concession, the Rudd Concession, with King Lobengula of the Ndebele. Rhodes and the BSA Company claimed that through this Concession, King Lobengula, a Ndebele, yielded to them Mashonaland, the land of the Shona. And on the basis of this clearly fraudulent concession, Cecil Rhodes and, indeed, the

British went on to disinherit the Shona of their Mashonaland and the resources therein. Apart from the mineral resources, which were so dear to Rhodes and his BSA Company, the British settlers, or the Pioneers we saw above, took over Shona agricultural and grazing lands. And the Shona's own agricultural and livestock livelihoods became bleak. And for many of them the only means of survival that again developed out of their precarious situation was to aid, as labourers and servants, the very British colonial settlers' enterprises which had deprived them of their own livelihoods. They became British settlers' farm labourers, company workers, and house servants. But the ill treatment and meagre wages their masters or employers gave them still left them miserable—impoverished slaves of sorts in their homeland. So much so that just like the Herero and the Nama in Namibia, the Shona, against all expectations, considering that they were regarded as beneficiaries of British colonisation in that it saved them from the Ndebele raids, revolted against their 'saviour' colonial masters in 1896.

Yes, while the British settler troops were all engaged in Matabeleland quelling a fierce Ndebele rebellion which became known as the Second Ndebele Rebellion, the Shona sounded their war cry, the Chimurenga, against the British even though they had made no prior preparations for war. It was purely a revolt out of pent up anger, frustrations, and hopelessness, as they descended on their masters with whatever tool, weapon, and object they could lay their hands on. Over 200 Europeans and Indians were killed by the time some settler forces were withdrawn from Matabeleland to come and contain Chimurenga—as the entire Shona revolt came be known. But even then they couldn't contain it. Unlike the Ndebele who were conventional warriors who engaged their enemies in open battle combat, the Shona employed guerrilla tactics of hit and hide that gave Chimurenga a distinct, indestructible nature. They would attack the settlers and quickly disappear into the numerous caves of Mashonaland. Not even reinforcements from the British Imperial Forces which came under a rabid Lieutenant Colonel Edwin AH Alderson (1859 – 1927) who, like General Lothar von Trotha in Namibia, ordered his troops to employ genocidal tactics of burning to ashes Shona homes, food barns, livestock, and poisoning their water-holes, managed to hound the Shona out of their caves and quell Chimurenga. To bring the revolt to a sure end and stem further loss of both Bantu African and British settlers' lives, it had to take an entire year and Cecil Rhodes himself personally pleading with both the Ndebele and Shona leaders, at the historic Matopo Indaba, to urge their fighters to lay down their weapons, while he and the British colonial settlers solemnly undertook to redress their grievances.

But dispossession, exploitation, and oppression of Bantu Africans were actually the marrow of British colonisation not only in Matabeleland and Mashonaland but throughout Bantu Africa. Although Bantu Africans elsewhere did not break into revolts on the scale of the Ndebele rebellions and Chimurenga, their ordeal was equally insufferable. For example, just like in Matabeleland and Mashonaland, Cecil Rhodes and his BSA Company acquired vast territories of Bantu African Luvale, Kaonde, Nkhoya, Tonga, and Ila of today's North Western, Western, and Southern provinces of Zambia through another fraudulent concession with another wily Bantu African ruler, Litunga Lubosi Lewanika, of the Bantu African Lozi people of Western Zambia. Without consulting the Luvale, Kaonde, Nkhoya, Tonga, and the Ila, Lewanika gave away their territories to Cecil Rhodes and his BSA Company for an annual subsidy of £200 and mineral royalties. Again on the basis of this deceitful acquisition, Cecil Rhodes and the BSA Company took to allocating or selling Bantu African lands to British settlers without regard for the inhabitants who were there. The British settlers in turn forcibly drove away the unfortunate inhabitants out of their homes and homelands.

Thus like the Ndebele and the Shona, the Tonga, Ila, and many more Bantu African groups were displaced into infertile tsetse-infested areas; And eking a living out of infertile dry lands proved a tall order for many of them. Their agricultural ventures grounded to a miserable end; and they who regarded their livestock as the mainstay of their economic lives as well as their mark of prestige, saw them wiped out by tsetse-borne diseases and lack of adequate pasture and water.

They were ruined.

In destitution and desperate for survival, many of them went back to their former homelands and begged their evictors, the British settlers, to have them back either as their poor 5-shillings-a-month labourers or as their impoverished tenants whose rent would be paid in form of free labour.

Indeed, having disinherited Bantu Africans of their homelands and resources, British settlers throughout their Bantu African colonies and protectorates still desperately wanted them back to provide cheap or free labour on their subsequent farms, mines, and commercial and residential plots. Quite alright they had access to funds with which to develop their newly acquired lands from Land Banks which their authorities took care to establish, but they still needed manual labour to have the actual works done. Tractors and many modern construction machines which of late are increasingly replacing manual labour were not yet in Bantu Africa, and for all the huge tracts of lands almost each one of them took up, the British settlers were very few in numbers to provide that much needed manual labour themselves. In fact, more than anything else, it was their desperate need for Bantu African labour that dreadfully mangled their colonisation of Bantu Africa.

Although some disinherited and displaced Bantu Africans willingly went back to British settlers to offer themselves up for cheap or free labour, a great majority of them deeply embittered with their disinheritance and displacement and, indeed, the devastating consequences which followed, did not want to have anything to do with the powerful invaders of their lands. And joining this group of disgruntled Bantu Africans who were unwilling to aid British colonial settlers and authorities with their schemes of taking over Bantu Africa for their own benefit were the many Bantu African groups who were still smarting from the defeats they suffered at the hands of the British in various wars and battles for their pillaging rights and spaces. This widespread indignation among Bantu Africans created acute shortfalls in the desperately needed Bantu African labour on British farms, mines, and firms. And as desperate situations call for desperate measures, British colonial authorities throughout Bantu Africa responded with neo-slavery of Bantu Africans. They slapped poll tax or head tax of about six shillings to £1 per month on every adult Bantu African. This was designed to compel all Bantu African adults to seek employment with either British colonial authorities or settlers who were the only source of that kind of money then.

The problem with this was that British settlers and colonial authorities only paid the eventual Bantu African labourers just enough to enable them pay the poll tax. And this was sort of taking away the meagre wages their right hands gave with their left hands. Clearly it rendered the toil of Bantu Africans under them virtual slavery—poll tax slavery. And making it really look like a case of slavers and slaves was the fact that until 1918 the British themselves were exempted from paying any such taxes although they earned far much more than Bantu Africans and it was their settlements, farms, enterprises, and infrastructure (public offices, schools, clinics, markets, streets, and so forth) that got constructed. Bantu Africans were restricted apartheid-style from British settlements, enterprises, and infrastructure.

Under such appalling circumstances, the poll tax inspired mass Bantu African tax evasion. And if mass Bantu African unwillingness to toil for the British made them respond with neo-slavery, mass Bantu African poll tax evasion managed to turn British colonial authorities into virtual 20th century slave and livestock raiders in Bantu Africa. Reminiscent of how Mwata Yamvo and his kilolos, we saw in chapter 2, dealt with noncompliant subjects vis-à-vis paying tribute to him and, indeed, reminiscent of how Europeans in general and Arabs secured Bantu African slaves from the 17th to the 19th century, British colonial authorities employed Bantu African chiefs and headmen to work with their Native Commissioners to hound and round up poll tax evaders. Bantu African chiefs and headmen were paid a tithe of the tax they helped get recovered otherwise they risked being deposed, and their chiefdoms and villages disbanded altogether and suffer severe personal penalties themselves for noncompliance with the orders and offers of the British colonial authorities. And the fate of the father of one of Bantu Africa's greatest freedom fighters, the late Nelson Mandela, aptly comes to mind here. Nelson Mandela's father, Gadla, was a headman who threw himself and his entire family into destitution for noncompliance with British colonial authority demands. *Nelson Mandela's* biographer, Martin Meredith, relates in Mandela's biography, *Nelson Mandela*:

Gadla's position as headman was dependant not only upon tribal lineage but upon the approval of White officials in the Cape colonial administration. After its annexation by Britain in 1885, Thembuland had come under the control of colonial magistrates who maintained a system of indirect rule through village headmen appointed to keep order among the local population as well as to represent their interests....

Well known for his stubbornness, Gadla fell into a minor

dispute over cattle with the local magistrate and refused to answer a summons to appear before him. Gadla took the view that the matter was of tribal concern and not part of the magistrate's jurisdiction. He was dismissed for insubordination, losing not only his government stipend but most of his cattle and his land and the revenue that went with them.

Thus, on one hand motivated by a few benefits that British colonial authorities threw at them and on another coerced by their colonial heavy-handedness, Bantu African chiefs and headmen hounded and captured poll tax evaders with a frenzy that had all the hallmarks of the 17th– 19th century slave and livestock raids conducted by their predecessors. And indeed, once captured the lot of poll tax evaders was hardly dissimilar to that of captured slaves and victims of livestock raiders. First, they had, like Nelson Mandela's father, their cattle, goats, pigs, and grain confiscated by colonial authorities. Secondly, they were committed to long durations of hard labour in colonial public works; a default of £1 earned one 4 months of hard labour. And then those men who proved hard to capture by fleeing their villages and chiefdoms leaving their wives behind, had their beloved wives themselves taken hostage impi-style—yes, remember the Zulu or Ngoni impis or the Ndebele amajaha taking their victims' wives as spoils of their raids. Only when their husbands gave themselves up were the poor wives set free.

In fear of such drastic reprisals, thousands and thousands of Bantu African males peacefully deserted their homes, wives, and children to go and toil under British settlers and colonial authorities in order to earn the required shillings with which to pay their poll taxes. And Bantu African livelihoods, farming, pastoralism, hunting, craftworks, et cetera, that had begun to revive when the same British fought and ended internecine Bantu African slave and livestock raids, were brutally nipped in the bud as their leading performers, Bantu African men, were sucked into yet another British or, indeed, European economic maelstrom right on the heels of the slave-trade.

Certainly, the epicentre of this new European economic maelstrom, the emphatic demonstration that the European colonisation of Bantu Africa was but another European economic maelstrom that fed on Bantu Africans, was not that of the exploitative British, nor that of the exterminating Germans, nor that of the inexorable Portuguese slave-drivers, but that of the one-man Belgian colonisation of the Congo Free State.

When King Leopold II of Belgium acquired the Congo Free State at the 1885 Berlin Conference that partitioned Africa, he immediately encountered daunting challenges in meeting the conditions he committed himself to at the conference. He had committed himself to not only develop his colony within a stipulated time but also to uplift the lives of Bantu Africans there and suppress the slave-trade and raids which were ravaging them, the most notorious Bantu African slave raiders and traders, Msiri and Tippu Tip, had their empires right in the Congo Free State. But having no Belgians in the Congo Free State, he could not have the Belgian government and people fund and undertake its development. Thus, like Cecil Rhodes with his Rhodesian territories, King Leopold engaged private companies and individuals to carry out development activities in the Congo Free State on his behalf for huge tracts of Congo lands he promised them. One such company, Companie du Congo pour le Commerce et l'Industrie (CCCI) undertook to construct a rail line from Kinshasa to Matadi on the Congo estuary for 577 acres of land per every kilometre constructed. And upon completion, CCCI got 314 685 acres of land in 1898. And another company, Compagne du Katanga, was granted ⅓ of the mineral-rich Katanga province for undertaking to develop it.

The problem with these arrangements was that Bantu Africans who inhabited the lands King Leopold awarded to the CCCI and Compagne du Katanga and others were not only forcibly displaced like the Shona, Tonga, Ila, and many others in British colonies, but they were also forcibly made to work for these companies under untold conditions, often without pay, tools, and food.

And to suppress Msiri's and his Bantu African Garanganze people's slave-trade activities, King Leopold engaged Belgian mercenaries. Once in the Congo Free State, these mercenaries recruited and armed thousands of Bantu Africans as their askari to (foot soldiers). The Belgian mercenaries and their askari routed Garanganze and killed Msiri in 1891. And from then on they had all Bantu Africans in the Congo Free State at their mercy; they did to them whatever they pleased. They plundered their villages for food to feed thousands of their askari, massacred the men folk who dared to resist, and took over their wives (impi-style) for their own sexual gratification.

And then King Leopold decided to put his rampaging mercenaries and their askari to economic use: he tasked them to collect for him huge quantities of ivory throughout his Congo Free State.

They again aggressively executed this task—they went about butchering elephants in the Congo Free State for the ivory and they also forcibly collected some of it from Bantu African hunters and traders they came upon. For a while King Leopold made a fortune out of a staggering amount of ivory his mercenaries and their askari procured him. Unfortunately, the world prices for ivory as compared to those of rubber fell tremendously.

Those rubber trees were equally naturally abundant in the

Congo Free State; King Leopold promptly and astutely directed his forces to switch from procuring him ivory to goading vast populations of Bantu Africans in the Congo Free State into collecting for him vast amounts of sap (rubber) from rubber trees in the forests. And all hell broke loose.

To meet King Leopold's required quantities of rubber; the Belgian mercenaries and their askari set quotas for individual Bantu Africans to reach in their sap collection per day. Failure to reach one's quota was punished by severe lashing with chiccotes (hippo skin whips), chopping off of one's limb or limbs, and, indeed, death—depending on the degree of failure to reach one's required quota. While the entire population, of about 20 million, of Bantu Africans in the Congo Free State, which King Leopold had pledged to uplift and protect from slavery at the Berlin conference, ended up effectively enslaved in his rubber forests, half of it ended up mutilated and dead from these atrocities his forces inflicted on them. And this, like the enormities of the slave-trade, again stirred the conscience of some Europeans. In one of the many European literary works that were published condemning the enormities of King Leopold's men in the Congo Free State, Arthur Conan Doyle (1859 – 1930), a Scottish physician and prolific writer whose many works include the famous Sherlock Homes detective stories, mourned, in his introduction to Edmund Morels book, Great Britain and the Congo: *"All cruelties of Alva in the Lowlands, all the tortures of the inquisition, all the savagery of the Spanish to the Caribs are as child's play compared with the deeds of the Belgians in the Congo."*

And Doyle went on to question poignantly:

The real values of those sonorous words Christianity and civilisation. What are they really worthy in practice when all the

Christian civilised nations of the earth can stand round, and either from petty jealousy or from absolute moral indifference can for many years on end see a helpless race, whose safety they have guaranteed, robbed, debauched, mutilated, and murdered, without raising a hand or in most cases even a voice to protect them?

But Europeans couldn't possibly commit any such cultural and moral aberrations, for by now, late 19th century and early 20th century, they had come to embrace the bastard of their thought and the ugliest of their modern philosophies—racism against Bantu Africans. As such in their eyes Bantu Africans were not worthy of Christian and civilised treatment and, in fact, to them Christianity and civilisation found Bantu Africans inadmissible. And for them to have saved Bantu Africans from the enormities of slavery and plunder which threatened to obliterate them was clearly a case of animal rights activists who rescue endangered animal species but do not in any way consider those animal species deserving of all the comfort, love, and humane treatment they themselves enjoy exclusively. Thus they saw nothing wrong with living a good life at the expense of a less deserving people; a people whose character had, in the words of Georg Hegel, one of their prominent 19th century thinkers we saw in Chapter 2, *"nothing harmonious with humanity;"* a people whose skin colour, facial features, and hair texture they found obnoxious.

David Hume had categorically stated that *"There scarcely ever was a civilised nation of that complexion, ... "*; a people whose languages, names, songs, and dances they said made God sick; a people whose beliefs and culture they branded pagan; and a people whose suffering their priests and bishops cited in the Christian scriptures as God-ordained.

Nonetheless, in some kind of mystical irony, it was this

virulent European colonisation of Bantu Africa, a European colonisation of Bantu Africa which sought to strip Bantu Africans of everything, including their humanity and lives, which, in fact, exposed their humanity for the whole world to see that they were nothing but uniquely, fully human. Yes, it was the storm of racial dispossession fanned by a twisted philosophy of the denigration of Bantu Africans which over stripped them so much that their unique complete humanity was unveiled for all to see. The more European colonialists dispossessed, impoverished, and obliterated Bantu Africans, the more they revealed something priceless and intrinsic about them all which no nation in the world, no matter how powerful or cruel, could take away from any of them—Ubuntu, their Bantu African humanity. And even when they were surely exterminated in Germany South West Africa (Namibia), the Congo Free State, South Africa, and so forth, their blood, flesh, and bones stood out from the dust so much so that every particle of it became replete with their Ubuntu DNA and thus made them and the land of their birth and death, Bantu Africa, equally inalienable.

And not only did the enormities of the colonisation of Bantu Africa bind Bantu Africans to their motherland inalienably, they also reconciled them with one another. Not until their dreadful colonisation by Europeans they were fiercely estranged into their ethnic groups. But when Europeans over stripped them all, they also saw each other's Ubuntu and recognised that whether it was that of a Ndebele, a Shona, a Ngoni, a Chewa, a Bemba, a Zulu, a Xhosa, a Lozi, or an Ila, it was one and the same Ubuntu. Indeed, when, for instance, the Shona revolted against the British who were but fighting their traditional enemies, the Ndebele, in the Second Ndebele Rebellion of 1896, something of historical significance and far-reaching political implications, not only in Southern Rhodesia, but throughout Bantu Africa and the world occurred: the Shona and the Ndebele, and Bantu Africans at large, as a people, as one and the same true nation, were reborn. They all transcended their ethnic animosity and saw a common enemy in European settlers and colonialists who were enslaving, exploiting, and dispossessing them all. And with this realisation came a common cause: to rid themselves of the enemy.

And Europeans themselves grasped and acknowledged this new awareness among Bantu Africans. They too began to see and treat Bantu Africans as one and the same regardless of their ethnic rivalries. Cecil Rhodes and the British, for instance, came down from the Matopo Hills Indaba that ended the 1896 joint Shona-Ndebele rebellion against them with a single colony of Southern Rhodesia (Zimbabwe) of both the Shona and the Ndebele instead of Mashonaland and Matabeleland. Likewise in 1911 they merged North Western Rhodesia and North Eastern Rhodesia into Northern Rhodesia (Zambia) and began to govern it as a single protectorate.

And thus would the European colonisation of Bantu Africa in a way retain some element of a lifeline for Bantu Africans even in its hurtful and twisted form. Certainly, without it Bantu Africa today, if by God's grace alone its people had managed to survive their fierce slave and livestock raids, would be balkanised into stunted ethnic republics: the Zulu republic, the Xhosa republic, the Shona republic, the Ndebele republic, the Lozi or Barotse republic, the Tonga republic, the Yao republic, the Chewa republic, the Lunda republic, the Bemba republic, the Nyamwezi republic, the Kikuyu republic, and so on and so forth. And here I must hasten to state that this acknowledgement, however, sharply contradicts Africa's foremost liberationist, Dr Kwame Nkrumah (1909 – 1972). In a speech to the OAU summit in Cairo in 1964, Dr Nkrumah said: *"By far the greatest wrong which the departing colonialists inflicted on us, and which we now continue to inflict on ourselves in our present state of disunity, was to leave us divided into economically unviable States which bear no possibility of real development.*"

But facts in our history and on the ground, especially in Bantu Africa, are not with our celebrated liberationist. Going by the fierce ethnic rivalries that plagued it, Bantu Africa alone, excluding the populace West Africa, and the warrior nations of the Horn of Africa, would have had over 200 republics had it not been for the colonial intervention, dreadful as it was. And history shows that in fact European colonialists even tried to go one better than the current Bantu African nation-states. Just as they merged their 4 separate colonies and numerous Bantu African homelands in South Africa into one republic of South Africa, they very nearly gifted Bantu Africans with another huge republic encompassing East, Central, and Southern Bantu Africa. Despite being widely seen by African liberationists as motivated by their selfish colonial interests, the British, for one, wanted all of Central and Southern Bantu Africa (Malawi, Zambia, and Zimbabwe) to be merged with all of East Bantu Africa (Tanzania, Uganda, and Kenya) into one viable economic, social, and political entity. And, indeed, just before they were swept out of power in Bantu Africa, the British had at least succeeded to federate Zimbabwe, Zambia, and Malawi into the Federation of Rhodesia and Nyasaland. And it was Bantu African liberationists themselves who resentfully took this federation apart in 1963. In his book, *End of Kaunda Era*, John Mwanakatwe (1926 – 2009), one of Zambia's prominent liberationists, decried:

Apart from the colonial power's policy of parsimony and racial discrimination over a period of seventy years, the imposition of the Federation of Rhodesia and Nyasaland on the unwilling people of Northern Rhodesia (Zambia) in 1953 had disastrous economic consequences. In ten years of the Federation preceding Independence, Zambia's own birth right had been whittled away for the benefit of Southern Rhodesia [Zimbabwe]. Money from the mines was being spent for the benefit of Southern Rhodesia. It was there that the roads were built, it was in Salisbury [Harare] and Bulawayo that buildings were constructed in an unprecedented economic boom.

Again, in no way is this surprising and deplorable. It merely affirms without doubt that what began as the ''corrective'' European colonisation of Bantu Africa turned out so insufferable that Bantu African liberationists could not help to throw the baby out with the bath water.

4

Liberation

When in the course of human events it becomes necessary for ... a people to dissolve the political bonds which have connected them with another and to assume among the powers of the earth the separate and equal station to which the Laws of Nature and Nature's God entitle them, a decent respect to the opinions of mankind requires that they should declare the causes which impel them to the separation.

—The Preamble to the American Declaration of Independence.

Just as a new mountain peak arises from an old volcano, the epoch-making Bantu African liberation struggle against European colonial rule essentially stemmed from their millennium-old liberation causes. The most fundamental of these were their pursuit of a better peaceful life, their quest for freedom from tyranny, servitude, and deprivation (liberty), and their search for lands and resources they could secure as their own (property rights).

To have suffered exterminations, slavery, and servitude and mass dispossession for almost an entire millennium, these liberation causes were, in fact, second nature to Bantu Africans. Their lives were a constant search for a better life, liberty and property rights. Indeed, when from as far back as 1 000 AD up to the 1600s they embarked on mass migrations from their common mighty empires such as the Luba-Lunda Empire, it was in pursuit of nothing else but peaceful lives, freedom from servitude and deprivation, and lands and resources they could secure as their own. And from then on, all through the slave-trade raids and the Mfecane, whenever and wherever they saw and felt their lives endangered, their liberty threatened, and their lands and resources insecure, they migrated to newer and newer lands until all of Bantu Africa was peopled. And with all of Bantu Africa peopled and thus with nowhere else to migrate to, it was still in pursuit of peaceful lives, liberty, and secured lands and resources that many of them asked for and, indeed, welcomed European colonisation, for as they suffered slave and livestock raids at the hands of mightier Bantu African groups, Europeans came in championing liberty, peace, and security to troubled Bantu Africans. Regrettably, as we have seen in the last chapter, Europeans for their own selfish ends mangled their promises of liberty, peace, and security into colonial genocides, neo-slavery, and mass disinheritance of Bantu Africans. And disappointed and disillusioned with European colonisation, Bantu Africans quickly reached down to their broken spirits and there salvaged their old pursuit of a better life, liberty, and secured own lands and resources. They erupted into liberation revolts against European colonisation in several European Bantu African colonies. The Shona, as we saw in the last chapter, caught the British unawares with Chimurenga in 1896; the Nama and the Herero in Namibia braved exterminations and rose against the ruthless Germans in 1902-04; the Yaka, Azande, Bashi, Babua, etc., repeatedly took up arms against the murderous Belgians in the Congo Free State from 1892 up to 1917; and Rev. John Chilembwe, for all his western education and Christian missionary upbringing, led his followers into a bloody uprising against the British in Nyasaland (Malawi) in 1915.

Now, it has to be reiterated from the start that these liberation revolts were essentially different from the numerous Bantu African wars fought against Europeans throughout Bantu Africa for pillaging rights and spaces we have seen at the beginning of the last chapter. Bantu African wars for pillaging rights and spaces were fought to resist colonial rule in order to perpetrate slave and livestock raids, and at a time when colonial rule had not even exhibited its atrocious nature. But Bantu African liberation revolts, uprisings, rebellions, etc., sought to right and possibly end a badly flawed colonisation of Bantu Africa, and only after it had utterly failed to live up to its billing.

Unfortunately, just as Europeans crushed all Bantu African resistance to colonisation, they comprehensively quashed all these nascent liberation revolts against them. So comprehensive and devastating were the defeats of early Bantu African liberationists that even the causes they were advancing were often terribly reversed or negated all together as more and more Bantu Africans, including themselves, ended up exterminated, dispossessed of their lands, resources, and property, and stripped completely of whatever few rights they might have had. Remember the extermination orders we saw in the last chapter issued against the

Nama and Herero people of Namibia by the German general,
Lothar von Trotha in 1902 – 04.

Still, Bantu Africans did not give up their liberation causes.
Acknowledging the military superiority of European colonialists, a
new crop of Bantu African leaders, many of them educated and
trained as teachers, clerks, preachers, journalists, etc., by the very
Europeans in missionary schools both in Africa and abroad
emerged and adopted a new non-confrontational way of advancing
Bantu African liberation causes. Like their compatriots everywhere
else in Africa and in the African Diaspora, they amicably began to
implore the all-powerful governing authorities themselves to
kindly use their power, knowledge, and resources to redress Bantu
African grievances. They and their compatriots in Africa and the
African Diaspora at large had been trained to believe that if they
politely and respectfully begged the European colonial authorities
to grant them and their people political, social, and economic rights
as opposed to violently confronting them, the European colonial
authorities, whom they had come to learn as men of honour and
good intent, would have no reason to deny Bantu Africans those
rights. The learned Dr William Sanders Scarborough (1852 –
1926), the first African American classical scholar and one of the
leading advocates of this approach advised:

*Interracial, like international questions must be settled, if ever
really settled, not by violence but by reason. My advice to
[Africans] would be to rise gradually but invincibly. I would tell
them to make such intellectual and moral progress, and such
progress in manners, that other peoples cannot help liking them.*

This respectful approach and ingratiating manner was formally

and famously adopted for all Africans on 23-25 July 1900 by 37
leading pan-Africanists, mostly from the African Diaspora in the
Americas and the Caribbean. Dr William Sanders Scarborough, we
have just seen above, was among them. They met in London for
what became known as the First Pan-African Conference. Meeting
as leading luminaries of the entire African race the world over,
hence the term pan-African, they endeavoured to spearhead a
negotiated liberation of all Africans from European oppression. A
memorable long communiqué they made the illustrious African-
American educator, historian, and writer, Dr W.E.B. Du Bois
(1868 – 1963) author at the end of their deliberations tells it all:

TO THE NATIONS OF THE WORLD.

*In the metropolis of the modern world, in this the closing year of
the Nineteenth Century, there has been assembled a Congress of
men and women of African blood, to deliberate solemnly upon the
present situation and outlook of the darker races of mankind.*

*The problem of the Twentieth Century is the problem of the
colour line, the question as to how far differences of race, which
show themselves chiefly in the colour of the skin and texture of the
hair, are going to be made, hereafter, the basis of denying to over
half of the world the right of sharing to their utmost ability the
opportunities and privileges of modern civilisation.*

*To be sure, the darker races are today the least advanced in
culture according to European standards. This has not, however,
always been the case in the past, and certainly the world's history,
both ancient and modern, has given many instances of no
despicable ability and capacity among the blackest races of men.*

*In any case the modern World must needs remember that in
this age when the ends of the world are being brought so near*

together, the millions of black men in Africa, America, and the Islands of the sea, not to speak of the brown and yellow myriads elsewhere, are bound to have great influence upon the world in the future, by reason of sheer numbers and physical contact.

If now the world of culture bends itself upwards, giving Negroes and other dark men the largest and broadest opportunity for education and self-development, then this contact and influence is bound to have a beneficial effect upon the world and hasten human progress.

But if, by reason of carelessness, prejudice, greed, and injustice, the black world is to be exploited and ravished and degraded, the results must be deplorable, if not fatal, not simply to them but to the high ideals of justice, freedom, and culture which a thousand years of Christian civilisation have held before Europe.

And now, therefore, to these ideas of civilisation, to the broader humanity of the followers of the Prince of Peace, we, the men and women of Africa in World Congress assembled, do now solemnly appeal:

Let the world take no backward step in that slow but sure progress which has successively refused to let the spirit of class, of caste, of privilege, or of birth, debar from life, liberty, and the pursuit of happiness a striving human soul.

Let not mere colour or race be a feature of distinction drawn between white and black men, regardless of worth or ability.

Let not the natives of Africa be sacrificed to the greed of gold, their liberties taken away, their family life debauched, their just aspirations repressed, and avenues of advancement and culture taken from them.

Let not the cloak of Christian missionary enterprise be

*allowed in the future, as so often in the past, to hide the ruthless
economic exploitation and political downfall of less developed
nations, whose chief fault has been reliance on the plighted faith of
the Christian church.*

*Let the British Nation, the first modern champion of Negro
freedom, hasten to crown the work of Wilberforce, and Clarkson,
and Buxton, and Sharpe, Bishop Colenso, and Livingstone, and
give, as soon as practicable, the rights of responsible government
to the Black colonies of Africa and the West Indies.*

*Let not the spirit of Garrison, Phillips, and Douglas wholly
die out in America; may the conscience of a great Nation rise and
rebuke all dishonesty and unrighteous oppression toward the
American Negro and grant to him the right of franchise, security of
person and property, and generous recognition of the great work
he has accomplished in a generation toward raising nine million of
human beings from slavery to manhood.*

*Let the German Empire and the French Republic, true to their
great past, remember that the true worth of colonies lies in their
prosperity and progress, and justice, impartial alike to black and
white, is the first element of prosperity.*

*Let the Congo Free State become a great central Negro state
of the world, and let its prosperity be counted not simply in cash
and commerce, but in the happiness and true advancement of black
people.*

*Let the Nations of the world respect the integrity and
independence of the free Negro States of [Ethiopia], Liberia, Haiti,
etc., and let the inhabitants of the states, the independent tribes of
Africa, the Negroes of West Indies and America, and the black
subjects of all Nations take courage, strive ceaselessly, and fight
bravely, that they may prove to the world their incontestable right*

to be counted among the great brotherhood of mankind.

Thus we appeal with boldness and confidence to the Great powers of the civilised World, trusting in the wide spirit of humanity and the deep sense of justice of our age, for a generous recognition of the righteousness of our cause.

Sadly all this elaborate appeal fell on deaf ears. From 1900 onwards, Europeans intensified their oppression of Africans as they sought to firmly establish colonial rule in most parts of Africa. Henry Labouret (1878 – 1959), a French colonial administrator, succinctly observed: "At the present time, the Pan-Negro movement born in the New World scarcely seems to menace the white hegemonies in Africa. It is clearly premature."

Compounding the problem for pan-African leaders and, indeed, that of their missionary educated counterparts, say, in Bantu Africa was the fact that they over indulged themselves in seeking European favour at the expense of stirring the vast majorities of their illiterate African masses into liberation movements. Even in the African Diaspora in the Americas and the Caribbean where the African masses had attained a significant level of basic education to comprehend pan-African leaders, the masses were divorced from their activities and pronouncements. Having been long initiated into black liberation movements with mass-gripping, radical calls such as Paul Cuffe's "Back to Africa," Bishop Henry M. Turner's "Africa for the Africans, *"and George Charles of Topeka's "United States of Africa,"* they were considerably alienated by pan-African leaders who seemed too bent on seeking their own assimilation into European societies rather than the liberation of all their people. And about the former, Dr W.E.B. DuBois was quite candid. Elated at being accorded noble treatment and honour by several of their noble and honourable English hosts during and after the 1st Pan-African Conference, he crowed:

On Monday, the 23rd of July, the Conference was invited to a five o'clock tea given by the Reform Cobden Club of London in honour of the delegates, at its headquarters in the St. Ermine Hotel, one of the most elegant in the city. Several members of Parliament and other notables were present. A splendid repast was served, and for two hours the delegates were delightfully entertained by the members and friends of the club.

At 5 o'clock on Tuesday a tea was given in our honour by the late Dr Creighton, Lord Bishop of London, at his stately palace at Fulham, which has been occupied by the Bishops of London since the fifteenth century. On our arrival at the palace we found his Lordship and one or two other Bishops, with their wives and daughters, waiting to greet us. After a magnificent repast had been served we were conducted through the extensive grounds which surround the palace. Prof DuBois, M. Benito Sylvain, Messrs Downing and Calloway, Miss Jones and others moved about the palace and grounds with an ease and elegance that was surprising; one would have thought they were "to the manor born." We found the Lord Bishop not only a brilliant scholar and profound thinker, but an affable Christian gentleman. I am sure our visit to the palace will be long remembered by the delegates as one of the most pleasant in their history.

Through the kindness of Mr Clark, a Member of Parliament, we were invited to tea on Wednesday, at 5 o'clock, on the terrace of Parliament. After the tea the male members of our party were admitted to the House of Commons, which is considered quite an honour; indeed, the visit to the House of Parliament and the tea on the Terrace was the crowning honour of the series. Great credit is due our genial secretary, Mr H. Sylvester Williams, for these social functions.

Miss Catherine Lumpey, of London, said she was glad to come in contact with the class of Negroes that composed the Pan-African Conference, and wished that the best and most cultured would visit England and meet her citizens of noble birth, that the adverse opinion which had been created against them in some quarters of late by their enemies might be changed.

I am glad that so many of our ministers, educators, and other members of the professional classes are making annual visits to Europe. Such visits are helpful to our cause. The Pan-African Association and the Afro-American Council, if efficiently officered and wisely managed, can do much for the amelioration of persons of African descent throughout the world, provided that they are supported in their work by the better classes of our people. Without such co-operation they are sure to fail.

And if the American luminaries who masterminded the independence of the USA from Britain and, indeed, composed the American Declaration of Independence in 1776 had exhibited such ingratiating manner towards the British as did Dr W.E.B. DuBois and his "best and most cultured class of Negroes that composed the Pan-African Conference," Americans would sure be still British subjects. In any case, for nearly 20 years after their 1st Pan-African Conference, Dr W.E.B. DuBois and his elite colleagues did indeed fail to sustain their Pan-African movement nor organise another treat of a pan-African conference which would have seen them rub shoulders and sip tea with Europe's nobility *"like the manor born."* It's impossible to tell whether this was due to lack of support "in their work by the better classes of [African] people," as Dr DuBois himself had warned, or something else. But it was well after the

First World War in 1919 that they held the 2nd Pan-African Conference and only on the side-lines of the post-World War I Versailles Peace Conference (aka the Paris Peace Conference) to which they were invited to represent all Africans.

Thus Africans throughout the world went through the First World War, an epic event in all human history into which they were helplessly sucked, with no particular African leadership. Quite right by 1912, two years before the First World War, some educated Bantu Africans in Bantu Africa, South Africa to be precise, founded the celebrated African National Congress (ANC). But these founders of the ANC were no different from the elite DuBoisian pan-Africanists. They did not then envisage themselves and their organisation leading Bantu Africans to liberation; using the ANC to pursue Bantu African liberation causes or as Monsieur Labouret put it "to menace the white hegemonies in [South] Africa" wasn't on their agenda; they were the exact opposite of Nelson Mandela, Walter Sisulu (1912 – 2003), Oliver Tambo (1917 – 1993), and colleagues who assumed the leadership of the same ANC some 4 decades later to specifically *menace the white hegemonies.*" Describing the founders of the ANC in Nelson Mandela's biography, *Nelson Mandela*, Martin Meredith writes:

The founders of the ANC were mostly conservative men, schooled in the Christian tradition, respectful of authority and concerned largely with their own position in society. When they gathered on a sweltering day in January 1912 in a community hall in a black location in Bloemfontein, formally dressed in suits, frock coats and top hats and carrying furled umbrellas, their main objectives, to defend African rights and to campaign against racial discrimination were notably modest. They were members of an African elite, brought up to believe in the inherent value of Western rules and anxious to prove their worth as loyal citizens.

*What had brought them together was not so much the urge to
agitate for advancement as the fear that their existing privileges
were under threat.*

So in the First World War Africans were effectively recruited
in massive numbers to fight for and defend acquisitive nationalistic
causes of their respective colonial masters; but all along there was
no African leadership to rally them all behind their own noble
liberation causes. And in that, their colonial masters' war, they put
up a remarkable performance, winning their respective masters
decisive battles and eventually the war. This stirred the conscience
of many Africans throughout the world who were left ruing that if
only it was their own noble liberation causes. And that many
Africans even died for purely egoistic causes of colonialists who
were but oppressing them and not their own, tormented them all
the more.

Consequently, the aftermath of the First World War for many
Africans the world over was a heightened general emotional drive
to radically advance their own liberation causes. By now there was
no doubt whatsoever that despite all their civilisation, power, and
capability, Europeans simply had no political will to attend to
Bantu African causes but their own. And the gentle appeals for
redress made to them by elite African leaders were now generally
considered useless. Bantu Africans and Africans the world over
had now to take a decisive course of action if their liberation
causes were to be realised. In a landmark ideological shift of sorts,
they conscientiously ditched imploring Europeans to attend to their
grievances and embraced the pursuit of self-determination.
Attaining self-rule or political, social, and economic independence
from Europeans began to be seen as the surest way of redressing
their grievances, the surest way of realising the illusive, primary
Bantu African or African liberation causes of better peaceful lives,

liberty, and secured own lands and prosperity. In giving a background to the liberation movement in Zambia, John Mwanakatwe, a Zambian liberationist himself, academic, and author, we have already seen above observed in *End of Kaunda Era:*

To the majority of the African people their humiliation, poverty, and suffering were all traceable to the lack of political influence. All their miseries such as racial discriminatory practices or inadequate school facilities for their children were traceable to the Africans' lack of political power.

Therefore, seeking autonomy infectiously gripped the imaginations of all Africans in Africa and in the African Diaspora as the key African liberation cause. Even the wheedling Dr W.E.B. Du Bois could not resist it. At the post-World War I Versailles Peace Conference he called for an autonomous post-World War I Africa divided at least into two or three states.

But the Versailles Peace Conference in 1919 again revealed to Africans and Dr W.E.B. DuBois the rude reality which had merely been obscured by the smoke and dust of the war, that despite coming out of a taxing, infernal war suffering severe fatigue, Europeans were strong enough to maintain and tighten their oppressive grip on Africa. The victorious European powers who gathered at that conference stood resolute for further colonialism as not a single one of them showed any room for letting up its hold on Africa. Only Germany, the defeated European power, was expelled from Africa, as part of reparations imposed on him. Left to help themselves to crumbs, allowed to table their post-war African demands in the light of forestalled demands for African autonomy, Dr W.E.B. DuBois and his fellow pan-Africanists as African representatives only managed to fall back on their usual tepid pronouncements. They demanded an end to colonial misrule, equality between Africans and Europeans, and proposed the internationalisation of all former German colonies in Africa.

But even these modest pan-African demands were totally disregarded by European powers at the Versailles Peace Conference. They upheld colonial misrule as the most effective way of getting the best out of Africans. They allowed colonisation to continue thriving on the denigration of Africans; and they divided up Germany's former colonies among themselves like plunderers sharing loot. Britain snapped up Tanganyika (mainland Tanzania) and German South West Africa (Namibia). France grabbed Chad, Central African Republic, Congo (Brazzaville) and Gabon. Belgium took up the diminutive Rwanda-Urundi (Rwanda and Burundi); and they split up Kameron (Cameroon) into Cameroons and Cameroun between Britain and France respectively and Togoland into Togo for France while Britain merged its portion of Togoland with its Gold Coast colony (Ghana).

The victorious European powers dealt Africans and their now key liberation cause of self-determination a severe blow. But rather than put out their smouldering liberation spirit, they only helped to fuel it into a fiery liberation movement complete with a fiery leader who not only fired the imagination of the African masses throughout the world but, at last, really managed to menace "the white hegemonies in Africa." That fire-brand of an African liberation leader was no other than the immortal Marcus Mosiah Garvey, Jr. (1887 – 1940).

Marcus Garvey was a Jamaican born African who, while living in the USA, succeeded to turn all the pent up African indignation against imperialism into a formidable African liberation movement. Unlike Dr W.E.B. DuBois who courted Africa's "better classes" into his pan-African 'assimilation' movement, Garvey rose as an enterprising and charismatic man of the masses. To the excitement of the long oppressed but agitated African masses throughout the world, he proclaimed *"the Renaissance of the Black Race!"* and roused them from political, social, and economic paralysis with uplifting slogans such as *"Up, you mighty Race! Africa Awake!"* And to back his proclamations and rousing slogans, to walk the talk, as they say, he helped establish African enterprises such as the famous Black Star Line, a shipping line, vying to replace European enterprises in Africa but at the same time to finance his liberation efforts. Then he set up the Universal Negro Improvement Association (UNIA) to propagate his ideas and programmes for the world-wide African liberation he envisaged. And aware that Europeans would not let go of Africa without a fight, he seriously began to raise an army, which he called the African Legion, with a view of liberating Africans by force if it came to that. Still, it never escaped his mind that the most formidable combatants for the African liberation were the African masses themselves; to this end he established an effective line of communication between him, 'the commander-in-chief,' and the rank and file of the African masses by publishing in English, French, and Spanish a weekly newspaper, The Negro World, and a daily, The Negro Times.

In a long speech in New York City on 25 November, 1922 designed to spell out both his and the UNIA's objectives in no uncertain terms, Marcus Garvey, memorably said:

Under the leadership of the UNIA we are marshalling the 400 000 000 Negroes of the world to fight for the emancipation of the race and of the redemption of the country of our fathers....

We represent a new line of thought among Negroes....

We are determined to unite the 400 000 000 Negroes of the world for the purpose of building a civilisation of their own....

We are looking toward political freedom in the continent of Africa, the land of our fathers....

If we have been liberal minded enough to give our life's blood in France, Mesopotamia, and elsewhere, fighting for the white man, whom we have always assisted, surely we have not forgotten to fight for ourselves, and when the time comes that the world will again give Africa an opportunity for freedom, surely 400 000 000 black men will march out in the battle plains of Africa, under the colours of the red, the black, and the green...We shall march out in answer to the cry of our fathers, who cry out to us for the redemption of our own country, our motherland, Africa....

For how can man fight better than by knowing that the cause for which he fights is righteous? How can man fight more gloriously than by knowing that behind him is a history of slavery, a history of bloody carnage and massacre inflicted upon a race because of its inability to protect itself and fight? Shall we not fight for the glorious opportunity of protecting and forever more establishing ourselves as a mighty race and nation, never more to be disrespected by men [?] Glorious shall be the battle when the time comes to fight for our people and our race.

We should say to the millions who are in Africa to hold the fort, for we are coming, 400 000 000 strong.

For many Africans in Africa and in the African Diaspora, Marcus Garvey was surely their long awaited liberator. They rallied to him and his proclamations; and they fomented with his rousing ideas, so much so that now "the white hegemonies in Africa" felt menaced. *"The white hegemonies in Africa"* began to curtail his growing influence with a series of draconian measures. Vincent Bakpetu Thompson in his book, *Africa and Unite*, recounts:

Garvey's newspaper, the Negro World, was banned [by imperialists], and heavy penalties were imposed on people found reading or even possessing copies of it. The punishment in certain colonial territories for possessing The Negro World was five years imprisonment with hard labour; in Dahomey [Benin] it was life imprisonment. The paper was also suppressed in Trinidad, British Guyana, Barbados, in the West Indies, and all French, Italian, Portuguese, Belgian, and some British colonies in Africa.

Tragically, helping the imperial enemy to considerably frustrate and undermine Marcus Garvey's growing African liberation movement was no less a person than our very own elite Dr W.E.B. Du Bois. Out of a subtle sibling rivalry of sorts, Dr DuBois developed intense hatred for Marcus Garvey and his liberation movement. In his own words quoted from his book, *Dusk of Dawn*, he was "naturally hurt" that Garvey's fiery and mass-gripping African liberation movement *"made difficult further effective development of [his] Pan-African Congress idea."* And in an article entitled 'Lunatic or Traitor' in The Crisis, the official magazine of the illustrious National Association for the Advancement of Coloured People (NAACP), a US African-American civil rights organisation, Dr DuBois castigated Garvey: "Marcus Garvey," he wrote, *"is, without doubt, the most dangerous enemy of the Negro race in America, and the World. He is either a traitor or lunatic."*

Yet haunted by Marcus Garvey's authentic and pragmatic African liberation ideas, Dr Du Bois could not help painfully admit, in another edition of The Crisis, that:

Shorn of its bombastic exaggeration, the main lines of the Garvey plan are perfectly feasible. What he is trying to say and do is this: American Negroes can, by accumulating and ministering their own capital, organise industry, join the Black Centres of the South Atlantic by commercial enterprise and in this way ultimately redeem Africa as a fit and free home for black men.

Nevertheless, according to Amy Jacques Garvey (1895 – 1973), Garvey's second wife, in her book, *Philosophy and Opinions of Marcus Garvey*, Dr Du Bois personally sabotaged all such endeavours by Garvey in Africa. During his 1924 visit to Liberia, which was then already an independent African state and thus Garvey's foothold in Africa, Dr Du Bois prevailed on President King of Liberia to sever all relations with Garvey whom he portrayed as bent on usurping power in Liberia.

And the US conspiracy machinery for mortifying prominent Africans, the FBI et al, was set on Garvey. It began to look for grounds on which to prosecute him. It even tried to no avail to have him nailed for bigamy by having him accused of co-habiting with Amy Jacques, who later became his second wife in 1922, while he was still married to Amy Ashwood Garvey (1895 – 1873), his first wife. And eventually in 1925 a US court handed him a five year jail sentence saying he had defrauded people over his Black Star Line project which endeavoured to return willing African Americans to Africa.

Following Garvey's imprisonment, his masses quickly became

disillusioned; and his movement and UNIA foundered.

In 1927, however, Marcus Garvey was released from jail. But he was in ill health; and he was immediately deported to Jamaica, the country of his birth. Still, he could not retrace his way with the masses. He eventually left Jamaica for England where he died of tuberculosis in 1940 in virtual obscurity.

And who so could give Marcus Garvey a contrite tribute than his greatest '*sibling*' rival, Dr W.E.B. DuBois. "*Garvey*," wrote Dr DuBois in his book, *Dusk of Dawn*, "*was an extraordinary leader of men.... My first effort was to explain away the Garvey Movement and ignore it; but it was a mass movement that could not be ignored....*"

However, for a more profound tribute to the immortal Marcus Garvey we probably have to turn to another immortal son of Africa and one of Garvey's own disciples, Dr Martin Luther King Jr., (1929 – 1968), the legendary African-American civil rights leader. Upon laying a wreath on Garvey's shrine in Jamaica on 20 June 1965, Dr King told the audience in attendance that:

Marcus Garvey was the first man of colour to lead and develop a mass movement. He was the first man on a mass scale and level to give millions of Negroes a sense of dignity and destiny, and make the Negro feel he was somebody.

Indeed, rivals and enemies alike may have succeeded to subdue Marcus Garvey, but none of them could wipe out his ideas in numerous latent Garveyites across the African continent and the African Diaspora. Garvey's radical liberation ideas had taken deeper root and meaning in many young African intellectuals, activists, and leaders both in Africa and in the African Diaspora. Martin Luther King Jr., we have just seen above; Malcolm X (1922 – 1965), who championed Black Nationalism in the USA and whose parents—Earl and Louise Little—actually met at a Marcus Garvey UNIA convention in Montreal, Canada; founding leaders of independent African states such as Kwame Nkrumah of Ghana, Jomo Kenyatta of Kenya, Julius Nyerere (1922 – 1999) of Tanzania, Leopold Sedar Senghor (1906 – 2001) of Senegal, Patrice Lumumba (1925 – 1961) of the Democratic Republic of Congo, and Anton Lembede (1914 – 1947), the radical South African youth leader who inspired the formation of the ANC's Youth League from which Nelson Mandela, Oliver Tambo, and Walter Sisulu rose to transform the then elitist ANC into a radical mass African party, all and many more influential Africans lit their torches of African liberation from Marcus Garvey's fiery liberation ideas. And soon after his death they all burst on the African and world political scene igniting listless liberation and civil rights movements in their respective countries with electrifying Garveyian liberation ideas.

And while it may have been practically difficult for Marcus Garvey himself who was in the Diaspora to sustain his influence among the African masses in Africa, for instance, most of his disciples took to the African liberation movement with an added advantage of being from among the African masses. They mobilised their masses into forces of liberation with natural ease. Under their close guidance and instructions, Africans in the 1940s fermented with increased political consciousness and activism. This culminated in the mushrooming of African Welfare Societies.

The purported aims of these welfare societies were to promote their members' economic and social wellbeing and "to build brotherhood and friendship among Africans," as read the constitutions of various welfare societies in Northern Rhodesia

(Zambia) such as the Mwenzo Welfare Association and the Chinsali African Welfare Association to which Kenneth Kaunda and Simon Kapwepwe (1922 – 1980), who became Zambia's founding leaders, were both members. But in essence welfare societies in Africa were hotbeds of liberation activities. And as African political agitation for self-rule intensified, many welfare societies rapidly and openly transformed themselves into African political parties that championed the cause of self-rule. This was even more so in the wake of the 1941 Atlantic Charter—signed in the heat of World War II by Great Britain's Prime Minister, Winston Churchill (1874 – 1965), and President Franklin D. Roosevelt (1882 – 1945) of the USA-- which proclaimed to *"respect the right of peoples to choose the form of government under which they live; and [wished] to see sovereign rights and self-government restored to those who [had] been forcibly deprived of them."*

To a large extent the 1940s marked a real turning point for the African liberation movement; not only because of the Garveyites' unmistakable influence, but also because of the tremendous impact world events such as the Second World War made on Africans. Other than the clearly impelling Atlantic Charter, the 1939 – 1945 World War II itself provided Africans a huge, fresh impetus to assertively advance their own liberation causes. Like the First World War, the Second World War wrenched Africans from their own causes to fight for those of their colonial masters. And this time almost all of their colonial masters were pitted against a vengeful Adolf Hitler's NAZI Germany and his few allies—Italy, Holland, Japan, and some Slavic States.

Germany was heading for a crushing victory over the Allies— Britain, France, the Soviet Union, China, etc. When at the close of 1941, December 8, 1941, the USA decided to come to the aid of the Allies to dramatically dispel their worst nightmare since the

Barbarian invasions, the Allies were on the verge of conceding a grievous defeat. So fighting beside their falling masters, many Africans lost their lives in the Second World War, much more than in the First World War. Thus widespread anger swept among Africans for again dying for causes that were not really theirs; and once more, they were stung into advancing their own liberation causes. And again just as after the First World War, they expected little opposition from their masters whom they hoped to concentrate on surviving the ravages of a monstrous war— especially this time when Germany had left them gasping for life under piles of rubble.

But again Africans had miscalculated the repercussions of their masters' enervation. Europeans desperately needed colonialism as much as the Marshal Plan to rise from the rubble, to fully survive the Second World War; they needed African cheap labour and cheap raw materials to have themselves back on the track of progress. In January 1948 the British Foreign Secretary, Ernest Bevin (1881 – 1951), openly admitted in the House of Commons that:

Colonies are large primary producers.... The other two great world powers, the United States and the Soviet Russia have tremendous resources. There is no need of conflict with them in this matter at all. If Western Europe is to achieve its balance of payments and to get a world equilibrium, it is essential that these resources should be developed and made available.

In fact, Bevin was not necessarily the first to openly smother African hopes for liberation in the 1940s. Winston Churchill, the British Prime Minister himself, had by September 1941 already emphatically exempted Africans and other European colonial subjects from the right of self-government. This is what he told the British House of Commons:

At the Atlantic meeting we had in mind primarily the restoration of the sovereignty, self-government, and the national life of states and nations of Europe now under the NAZI yoke.... So that is quite a separate problem from the progressive evolution of self-governing institutions in the regions and peoples which owe allegiance to the British Crown.

But all such colonial obstinacy in the 1940s, especially after the Allies' own successful and exemplary expulsion of NAZI Germany from all its colonies and occupied territories, was rowing into a storm. Colonised peoples throughout the world were now convinced that colonialism, be it by the British, Belgians, or NAZI Germans, was evil and totally unacceptable in the new world order which both the Atlantic Charter and subsequently the United Nations Organisation were trying to promote. From this moral fortress African liberation leaders too had, by 1945, resolved to root out colonialism in Africa at all cost. In 1945 about 300 delegates representing various African liberation movements and pan-African organisations convened in Manchester, England, to not only warn imperialists that they were now taking their people onto a war path against colonialism but also to sound a battle-cry for their people themselves and urge them to dress for battle. Although the compliant Dr W.E.B. DuBois was in attendance and co-chaired this congress to even earn it the title of the 5[th]DuBoisian Pan-African Congress, he was only a figurehead. The leading luminaries at this congress were largely burgeoning Garveyites: Kwame Nkrumah and George Padmore (1903 – 1959), joint secretaries; T. Ras Makonnen (1900 – 1983), treasurer; Peter Abrahams (b. 1919), publicity secretary; and Jomo Kenyatta, assistant secretary. And nothing said volumes that this was clearly a Garveyian conference than its pronouncements which came out as though they had been scripted by Marcus Garvey himself:

DECLARATION TO THE COLONIAL POWERS.

If the Western world is still determined to rule mankind by force, then Africans, as a last resort, may have to appeal to force in the effort to achieve freedom, even if force destroys them and the world.

We are determined to be free. We want education. We want the right to earn a decent living; the right to express our thoughts and emotions, to adopt and create forms of beauty. We demand for black Africa autonomy and independence.... We are unwilling to starve any longer while doing the world's drudgery.... We will make the world listen to the facts of our condition. We will fight in every way we can for freedom, democracy, and social betterment.

DECLARATION TO THE COLONIAL PEOPLES.

We affirm the right of all colonial peoples to control their own destiny. All colonies must be free from foreign imperialist control, whether political or economic.

The peoples of the colonies must have the right to elect their own Governments, without restrictions from foreign powers. We say to the peoples of the colonies that they must fight for these ends by all means at their disposal.... The Fifth Pan-African Congress therefore calls on workers and farmers of the colonies to organise effectively. Colonial workers must be in the front of the battle against imperialism. Your weapons—the strike and the boycott—are invincible…. We also call upon the intellectuals and professional classes of the colonies to awaken to their responsibilities…. Today there is only one road to effective action—the organisation of the masses. And in that organisation the educated colonials must join. Colonial and subject peoples of the world, Unite!

No true DuBoisian Congress would have issued these militant pronouncements. As for Marcus Garvey, he must have turned in his grave to salute his disciples for honouring his spirit in that manner. And when colonial powers called their bluff by adamantly perpetuating colonialism, as we saw Ernest Bevin in 1948 above, they, the Garveyites, ably demonstrated that they were not merely parroting their great mentor but meant every word of their militant pronouncements. Cleverly targeting Europeans' openly declared interests in Africa—"raw materials, food, and resources," in Bevin's words—they set off their masses into invasive strikes, boycotts, riots, revolts, and general turmoil throughout the 1950s in a bid to render the unjust ways of exploiting them unviable. And the "white hegemonies in Africa," recoiled. They cried foul in their parliaments and courts of law accusing Africans of economic sabotage. And when they tried to spring back to vindictively bash down and snuff out the ardent liberationists, they only added fuel to the flames: Africans rapidly plunged onto the war path singing: "Moto, moto wayaka; motowayaka; moto wayaka*!" (The* fire, the fire has blazed; the fire has blazed; the fire has blazed!) They burned down bridges, schools, houses, churches, offices, shops, and crops of Europeans and their sympathisers. And when again they tried to appease them with piecemeal constitutional changes which only gave them minimal freedom and rights but still left them under the colonial yoke, they took up real arms in Kenya, Zimbabwe, Mozambique, Angola, Namibia, and South Africa (Umkhonto we Sizwe[5]), and launched full scale liberation wars which not only disrupted European economic interests but endangered many European lives considerably.

And in less than a decade of *moto* blazing unstoppably, the British in Kwame Nkrumah's Gold Coast (Ghana) capitulated to Africans. The Gold Coast became the first African colony to regain its independence from a colonial power, Britain, in 1957. And from then on regaining African autonomy was pressed home— after the Gold Coast many more European colonies in Africa, including Bantu Africa, successively attained the auspicious African liberation cause of African autonomy which both the African masses and the liberation leaders generally believed to underpin their three fundamental liberation causes of a better peaceful life, liberty, and secured own lands and property.

---

[5]The ANC's military wing whose military activities Nelson Mandela and his colleagues were mostly jailed for.

5

Betrayal

*Independence has not given the African masses back their land.
They are still without food or clothes. But now there is a
difference. Before independence basic realities were boldly and
visibly delineated. All conflicts were reduced to two polarities—
white was wealth, power, and privilege, black was poverty, labour,
and servitude. 'Remove the white man,' cried the nationalist
leaders, and the root cause of our troubles is gone.' Gone? Not
exactly! The peasants and workers are still the hewers and
carriers....*

---Ngugi Wa Thiong'o

That to all intents and purposes African autonomy implied that Africans had regained the power to determine what to do with their lives, freedom, and resources, the power to grant themselves their long sought after better peaceful lives, liberty, and secured own lands and property, and thereby alter their miserable lot in life and shape themselves a glorious destiny, no one but a complete cynic, let alone a non-African one, expected it to equally and horribly fail them just as the European colonisation of Africa, which had also promised them liberty and security, had done before it. Regaining independence was too big a golden opportunity for long suffering Africans to miss converting it into endless possibilities of marvellous lives which now lay before them all. Yet it was spectacularly missed, like a football star failing to convert a penalty when the opposing goalkeeper had long dived to the wrong side.

With power in their hands, leaders of independent African states chose to do with it the absurd and ignored the obvious. They abandoned their own people's long pursued fundamental liberation causes of better peaceful lives, liberty and secured own lands and property and delved into hazy ideological experiments. They experimented with communism, socialism, capitalism, and so forth while their people waited to regain their lands, liberty, and better lives European colonialism had taken away from them.

The first thing European colonialists did when they took the reins of power in Africa was to empower their own people, the Pioneers, settlers, Boers, *Prazeroes*, and so forth, with the very best lands and resources Africa could provide; and then they put at their disposal money (from Land Development Banks) and cheap (African) labour with which to exploit them and hence build themselves viable colonial economies which gave them enviable lives of opulence. Not so when African nationalist leaders came to power. They held on to the vast African lands, resources, and money claiming they were holding everything in trust for everyone as communism and socialism dictated. On the other hand they let European settlers keep their lion's share of the lands, resources, and wealth they mostly acquired by dispossessing and exploiting Africans as capitalism and the Truth and Reconciliation Commissions demanded. Long before South African Bantu African nationalist leaders could win themselves Nobel Prizes for this benevolence, Bantu Africa's staunchest liberationist, Kenneth Kaunda, is on record as having traversed his country, Northern Rhodesia (Zambia), in the early 1960s assuring Europeans that there would be no redress in a Bantu African led Zambia that would affect them economically. According to his contemporary, compatriot, and fellow liberationist, John Mwanakatwe, in his book, *End of Kaunda Era:*

Kaunda played an important role in creating confidence among Europeans in an African government which would eventually lead to political stability and economic prosperity. More than any other political leader, Kaunda toured the country and addressed many meetings mostly of European businessmen…. He was much in demand as a speaker at lunches and dinners organised by [European] businessmen or professional bodies.

Thus while European settlers were allowed to thrive on their ill-gotten lands and wealth, Africans, especially Bantu Africans were abandoned to fall back on their primitive 14th century devices: hoes, axes, goats, cows, poor overused patches of state or customary land, and, with luck, that is barring the common droughts, a seasonal good rainfall.

In 2007 President Nicolas Sarkozy (b. 1955) of France caused a racial storm when in his address to students at Senegal's Cheikh Anta Diop University deplored this self-induced plight of Africans. He said:

The tragedy of Africa is that the African man has not fully entered into history. The African peasant, who for thousands of years has lived according to the seasons, whose life ideal was to be in harmony with nature, only knew the eternal renewal of time, rhythmed by the endless repetition of the same gestures and the same words.

In this imaginary world where everything starts over and over again there is no place for human adventure or for the idea of progress....

The idea never came to the African to get out of this repetition and to invent his own destiny.

Ever so sensitive to racist overtones and gestures as Africans are, owing, undeniably, to a ferocious torrent of racist sentiment and actions they have suffered at the hands of Europeans, especially, as we have seen already in chapter 2, it is easy to treat Sarkozy's remarks as just another of them. Even the eminent Cameroonian scholar, Achille Mbembe (b. 1957) fell for that easy racist brand. He compared the remarks, which he dubbed *"violation by language,"* to the racist texts of 19th century Europe we have seen. And he scoffed: *"What credibility can we afford such gloomy words that portray Africans as fundamentally traumatised beings incapable of acting on their own behalf and in their own recognised interest?"*

But polemics aside, the haunting fact is that African nationalist leaders, incredibly oblivious to their own people's *"recognised interests"*, own secured lands and property, liberty, and better peaceful lives, never seized the opportunity independence provided to re-invent their destiny. At independence they should have *"fully"* led their people *"into history"* by not only reclaiming power but also the lands and fruits of their labour therein (wealth and property) they had been deprived of. And when today Julius Malema (b. 1981), the young leader of South Africa's newest political movement, the Economic Freedom Fighters, sounds as though he is advocating nationalisation in South Africa, he is simply saying in one way or another Bantu African South African leaders should have restored South African lands and wealth to individual Bantu African South Africans, as opposed to the South African state, for their freedom to be meaningful. But with the international community bestowing statesmanship and Nobel Prizes on them for falling in love with their defeated oppressors and exploiters, they thought it immodest to ever impart "the idea" into their people *"to get out of"* peasantry and servitude and become new landowners, factory owners, bank owners, and employers. And to paraphrase Sarkozy's statement and sterilise whatever racist overtones it may harbour, the tragedy of Africa is that of all people, African nationalist leaders, including Sarkozy's beloved Leopold Senghor of Senegal whom he quoted with unmistakable admiration throughout his thought-provoking address, are the ones who abandoned their people to the 14th century way of life of relying on nature's providence. At independence when Africans were supposed to rapidly restore parity with all other 20th century peoples, their nationalist leaders, like a bigoted football referee who orders a fouled player to resume his play where the foul was committed when despite it the player has already moved into a favourable scoring position, deliberately condemned them to resume their advancement where they left it 600 years ago when Europeans disrupted it with their Trans-

Atlantic slave-trade.

Interestingly, away from the simple reason of protecting European economic interests in their countries in order to uphold their international images, there was, and still is, something queer, almost superstitious, which made African nationalist leaders maintain Europeans at the helm of their countries' economies rather than let their own people replace them. (Africans in general, no matter their level of education and sophistication, are helplessly superstitious.) African leaders literally dreaded, and still dread, to be surrounded by millions of their rich people. They were, and still are, politically uncomfortable with their masses or any of their people owning real stakes such as lands, property, and wealth in their countries' economies. For them there is no danger for a few foreigners or foreign investors to own a number of significant assets in their countries but not any of their people, let alone millions of them owning millions of assets. They consider that tantamount to yielding all ownership, including power, to any of their people or to their masses whom they sometimes deeply loathe out of tribal jealousies or so.

On 19 February, 2013 when I was drafting this book and this very chapter, President Michael Sata of Zambia stunned his nation with his outbursts of anger upon discovering that Hakainde Hichilema (b. 1962) a Bantu African Zambian businessman and leader of one of Zambia's leading opposition parties, the United Party for National Development (UPND), was, by Zambian standards, very wealthy. Citing him and his wealth as a danger not only to Zambia but the entire Commonwealth, he even went out of his way to order a release to the entire nation and the Commonwealth contents of a dossier his intelligence officers had compiled about Hichilema's properties and assets. President Sata, as quoted by his own state newspaper, the *Times of Zambia*, said— in reference to Hichilema who had earlier invited the

Commonwealth to come to Zambia to check on President Sata's government human rights violations, *"I am glad that Mr Hichilema has invited the Commonwealth, we will show them this document."* And he passed a dossier around which in part laborious read:

Preliminary investigations indicated that Mr Hichilema had ranches, which made him to emerge as one of the leading suppliers of beef to Zambeef PLC in the country.

The ranches had 90, 000 cattle in Central and Southern Provinces valued at [$ 72, 000].

The ranches were divided as: four in Choma District, operating as H.H. Farm and Blukes Farms whose property number was F/2295/A and have about 20, 000 animals.

One ranch located in Namwala District, operating under the name of H.H. Farms whose property number was L/2482/m and had about 16, 000 animals.

Another farm in Kalomo District operating as H.H. Farms B. William whose property number was F/821/A and had 35, 000 animals while three ranches in Kalola, Chibombo District, whose property numbers were F/1604/A, F/2270/A and F/9184 had 35, 000 animals.

Mr Hichilema had four bank accounts with Zambia National Commercial Bank (ZNCB), with the ZIMCO account in liquidation bearing account number 0030410001474, based at Lusaka's Business Centre branch having US $ 5,385.86....

Mr Hichilema had shares in private companies which included, ALS Capital, a bureau de change based at Makuba House in Lusaka, Beef Up Zambia Limited, a marketing company based at Longolongo Road in Lusaka....

He also had other shares in prestigious Zambezi Sun International Hotels based in Livingstone, Pick 'n' Pay and Game Stores in Lusaka.

Others being Anglo-American Corporation and Elliott and Touche, an accounting firm based in Lusaka.

The Opposition leader had three houses in South Africa, two in England three in Lusaka's Kabulonga area and office blocks in Choma District....

Kenneth Kaunda, President Sata's close mentor who had him serve in his own government in various portfolios and now increasingly acts like Zambia's co-President by gracing every one of President Sata's state functions, was even more disdainful of Zambian businessmen and property owners in general. He unleashed state investigators on any Zambian who happened to succeed to acquire and own a house, a shop, a vehicle, and let alone a farm or a ranch.

Recalling those awful days under Kaunda, Dora Siliya (b. 1970), a former Cabinet Minister in Zambia's Movement for Multi-party Democracy (MMD) government which ousted Kaunda from power, once wrote in an online publication, The Zambian Watchdog: *"Being seen to own property of any kind, even owning more than one TV set was enough ground to be investigated."*

Those who were found to be rich, by Zambian standards, like Hakainde Hichilema we have seen above, and in those days it was people like Valentine Musakanya, Edward Shamwana, and Yoram Mumba, Kaunda bluntly had them accused of plotting to overthrow his government and sentenced to death. Although he never actually had these men executed, he had them held in Zambia's maximum security prison, *Mukobeko,* indefinitely.

John Mwanakatwe in *End of Kaunda Era*, states: *"By 1970 Kaunda's attitude to Zambian businessmen had changed. He saw the upcoming Zambian entrepreneurs as a dangerous group."* Mwanakatwe goes on to say that when introducing the Matero Economic Reforms in Lusaka's Matero township in 1969, Kaunda openly expressed his apprehension about the then emerging Zambian entrepreneurs: *"How can we control this group at the same time allow them the freedom to exercise their initiative?"* He asked.

In his book, *Marx Money Christ,* Fr. Oswald Hirmer wrote: *"The rulers of the newly independent African countries are searching for their own way in the jungle of ideologies. Will they follow Marxism/Leninism or Capitalism?"* But as far as those "rulers of independent African states" were concerned even such a question was sheer political, social, and economic mumbo-jumbo, so much so that they could hardly choose either way. Jomo Kenyatta, Kenya's founding President stated that: *"We rejected both Western Capitalism and Eastern Communism and chose for ourselves a policy of positive non-alignment."* For them the real clear-cut question they faced at independence though unspoken was simply: to own or not to own? And this is the silent but inescapable question they could not help address themselves to. Haunted by the spectre of being overwhelmed by their own wealthy people, they all frantically chose not to own. And lest anyone thought this, their choice, strange, they resourcefully evoked African history and culture and argued that *'to own'* was un-African. *"We cannot accept material success as a way of life.... Our society is founded on spiritual democratic values,"* asserted Sarkozy's beloved Leopold Senghor of Senegal. And, as writes Fr. Hirmer, Julius Nyerere of Tanzania, Kenneth Kaunda of Zambia, Kwame Nkrumah of Ghana and many more nationalist African leaders all cemented their respective brands of African ideologies they came up with—Ujamaa, Humanism, Conscientism or

Communalism and so forth—and which frowned on '*to own*,' with the assertion that: "*In traditional African society everyone was rich or poor. All shared in the common wealth or misery.*"

Quite right for hundreds of years, even before the European intrusion, African rulers did not let Africans own lands, animals, and many fruits of their labour. They systematically dispossessed them in the name of loyalty and tribute to them and their kingdoms. But Africans deeply resented that. And it was out of that resentment that they embarked on the pursuit of the fundamental African liberation causes of liberty, secured own lands and property and better peaceful lives as expressed in their mass emigrations from their kingdoms, their deliberate courting of European colonisation, and eventually in the independence African nationalist leaders themselves presided over.

To own is a divine right. To own is to have a fulfilled life, to have required resources, food, comfort, peace of mind, dignity, respect, et cetera et cetera, to have and not to be in want. It is to have no poverty. Poverty is having nothing to own. And '*to own or not to own*?' is the original trillion dollar question. It is the fundamental question of all economics.

Whichever way a person or nation, through its leaders, chooses to answer this question decides that person's or nation's station in life. If an individual or a nation decides '*to own,*' an invisible natural law, some divine providence of sorts, affirms: "*To own, it is.*" And of necessity that individual or nation seeks wealth and eventually becomes wealthy. On the other hand if an individual or a nation decides '*not to own*,' that invisible natural or divine providence of sorts endorses: "Not to own, it is." And that individual or nation, as if cursed, will seek nothing and live in perpetual poverty.

To avoid being seen by their people that they had intentionally chosen for them *'not to own'* when they could have possibly and easily chosen *'to own,'* African nationalist leaders employed subtle ways of keeping their people poor or *"under control,"* as Kenneth Kaunda wanted. One of the major priorities of their new governments was to educate their people whom colonial governments had largely kept ignorant. To their credit after independence they succeeded to educate quite a sizable proportion of their people. But what they did to their educated people is outrageous. They denied them job opportunities commiserate with their education. Despite the many potential jobs which lay available in various fields of their developing nations such as manufacturing, construction, and industry, many graduates in such disciplines and more found themselves loitering the streets of their cities for many years hunting for their rightful jobs to no avail. Compelled by the instinct to survive the hardships of city life, especially if unemployed, they eventually took up odd jobs like sweeping the streets, car washing, street vending, charcoal burning and so forth and resigned themselves to a miserable life in the slums.

As though this was not by design—in order to keep their educated men and women down, so that they never make good in life and rise to challenge their positions of authority—they would often admit how scandalous this was, feign sympathy and concern, and adroitly absorb themselves of all blame citing the atrocious colonial legacy they were but unwilling to redress and a bad education system they had just put in place as the cause. Kenneth Kaunda in his book, *Letter to My Children,* moaned with treacherous candour:

A long and difficulty road lies ahead of our nation. In spite of all the efforts of Government and other agencies, I fear that many of our present generation of young people may never fulfil their potentialities. Their growth has been stunted by inherited evils it will take a long time to eradicate. A shanty town is hardly the setting in which personal fulfilment is likely to be fostered. The family trapped in poverty and ignorance can offer its children little stimulus other than a sense of bitter rebelliousness, of hate almost, that God, the Party, the Government, circumstance, or all four, have conspired to rob them of their rightful heritage.... It is a national scandal that so many of our young people fail to realise their potentialities. It weighs on my own conscience and I hope on the conscience of our nation. At time when our country has so many claims on its human resources, it is unthinkable that we should resign ourselves to a situation of wasted talent and energy either because educational opportunities are not available or because the products of our educational system cannot find creative openings for their gifts. A nation of matriculated road sweepers has little on which to congratulate itself.

It sounds harsh to label all such lamenting as totally insincere. But when you consider what the same leaders and their governments did to those *'lucky'* graduates whom they themselves ended up employing as civil servants—teachers and clerks, nurses and doctors, policemen and soldiers, agricultural officers and social workers and so forth—any sincerity in their laments peters out like morning mists. To equally impoverish their civil servants nationalist leaders begun by shirking to reward their skilled output claiming that doing so would endanger equality in their young nations. Here is Kenneth Kaunda again in his book, *Letter to My Children,* on rewarding skilled output or *"excellence,"* as he put it:

I have talked about the pursuit of excellence as a worthwhile goal which is both individually fulfilling and socially useful. But there is tension here which must be identified and, if possible, resolved. Does the pursuit of excellence conflict with one of the main drives of the main democratic State—the importance of equality? Can we be both equal and excellent too? This is a vital question. On the one hand we need those who can demonstrate excellence in many fields of endeavour, on the other, the mass of the people, quite rightly demand equality. To what extent then dare we favour the excellent without creating an aristocracy of talent—an elite which may form the basis of a new kind of class division? I have given much thought to this problem.

There is an old saying: 'You can't keep a good man down!' Unfortunately, our bitter experience of colonisation and racism has taught us that not only can elitist societies keep a good man down but in some cases they have kept a whole race down. So historically our first aim as a people has been to ensure equality....

So under the guise of fostering equality in their countries, they ended up paying their skilled manpower miserable wages that could only keep them alive but not buy for them houses, cars, farms or any other significant property. Medical doctors, clinical officers, teachers, policemen, and so forth found themselves in clamped two or three-roomed government-owned houses which had neither electricity nor running water. Like everyone else, indeed, that is *"the mass of the people,"* they walked or commuted to their places of work or any other destinations. Above all, at the end of such a trying service to their nations, they, like *"the mass of the people"* in their nations, had nothing to their names save one or two papers on which to draw their equally miserable pensions.

Now, if the aim of all this austerity towards skilled workers was really to foster equality, wouldn't endeavouring to uplift their poor compatriots, the masses themselves, to prosperity too, instead of impoverishing anyone for their sake, have achieved much desirable results? Why drag every one of their people into abject poverty when as liberationists they had fought to better their lives? Because *'to own'* is un-African, isn't it? As a matter of fact, African nationalist leaders did not end with impoverishing their skilled workers alone, but, astonishingly, they reached down to the very poor masses they intended to benefit with the impoverishment of their skilled compatriots and dragged them even further down into wretchedness.

To begin with, according to John Mwanakatwe, Kaunda's compatriot and former Cabinet Minister, African nationalist leaders, for all their tortuous concepts of equality, never really sought equality in favour of their poor masses. In *End of Kaunda Era,* Mwanakatwe reveals that:

No serious attempts were made by the new government to adopt policies which would have favoured rural dwellers in an effort to reduce disparity in rural and urban incomes. Five years later an urban worker's average [meagre] income was twice as much as the peasant farmer's income.

The poor unskilled African masses who made about 90% of their nations' populations did not only bear the full blunt of being abandoned to peasantry and into the hands of overbearing traditional rulers as in the times of old, but had the products of their toil taken away almost for nothing by African nationalist governments. Nationalist governments bought the cash crops they struggled to produce to raise money for their daily needs at terribly low fixed prices. So terribly low were the prices nationalist governments gave them that year after year of back-breaking toil they still failed to meet their basic necessities of life such as clothes, blankets, shoes, soap, salt, sugar, cooking oil, and so forth. Passing a verdict on Kenneth Kaunda's treatment of 'the mass of the people,' as he liked to call them, and in whose name he sought equality by suppressing the prosperity of his country's skilled manpower, John Mwanakatwe, again, wrote in *End of Kaunda Era*:

For many years from independence in 1964, the government did not provide attractive incentives for growing food crops such as maize, wheat, rice and so on. The farmers were given unfair prices which were often distorted by the dominance of price controls established by the government.... The Kaunda administration inflicted a death blow on farmers by the perpetuation of the colonial government's system of holding down food prices for the mining and urban sectors by paying them low prices.

As if to demonstrate what would have come of Zambia's peasant farmers had Kenneth Kaunda's government tried to help them out of poverty by at least giving them right prices for their crops, for a decade, 2001 – 2011, two of his successors, Levy Mwanawasa (1948 – 2008) and Rupiah Banda (b.1937), respectively gave them adequate government subsidised fertilisers and seeds; and suddenly their villages gleamed with iron-roofed houses and reconditioned Japanese vehicles. They recorded successive bumper harvests and, given fair prices for it, raised enough money, for the first time in their history, to not only meet their daily needs but also to buy their personal vehicles and build themselves bigger modern brick and iron-roofed houses, which unfortunately they now can't officially own just because they were built in customary lands which are still owned and arbitrarily controlled by their chiefs. And Zambia as a whole which perpetually used to suffer food shortages, a factor which greatly contributed to Kaunda's downfall, emerged as the region's food basket.

Admittedly, it took too long for nationalist leaders to be ousted. Some stayed in power for as long as three decades and some are, in fact, still in power. This gives an impression that they were greatly appreciated by their people. Far from it!

Almost from their inception nationalist governments were passionately detested by their people. Whatever they espoused and accomplished after assuming power had little blessings and appreciation from their people. Frankly, compared to colonial governments, they accomplished a great deal. They had many major roads tarred, long railways laid, better bridges constructed, bigger international airports built, outlandish and un-African skyscrapers erected, new hospitals and schools opened even in rural Bantu Africa. But all these developments had little impact in the lives of the vast majority of their people who had no means of utilising them. Over 90% of their people could not even conceive of ever setting foot in any of the freak skyscrapers their leaders had erected; they could neither dream of ever driving their own cars in their countries' new traffic-less tarred roads; boarding an aeroplane at their bigger international airports—they were realistic enough to know that not even their great grandchildren would do such a thing under their plight.

A tarred road or a rail line is like a mighty river that passes through one's village occasionally ferrying boats of all sorts laden with great goodies when all one does is watch and eventually die a miserable death in poverty. How then would one thank God for making that river pass through his village? Really, who remembers to thank God for the beautiful blue sky over our heads when underneath it we toil to our miserable deaths? How then would Bantu Africans, for one, praise their leaders for building universities for them when their degrees from those universities could not get them the desired jobs but only saw them join millions of their uneducated brothers and sisters in poverty?

Lest they were called ungrateful and un-resourceful, many educated and skilled Africans ingeniously found a way of passionately thanking their nationalist leaders. At a time their skills and services were greatly needed to develop their countries, they put patriotism aside and went to trade them for a decent living in Europe, Asia, Australia, and the Americas—much to their nationalist leaders' mystifying chagrin, but a skilled man does not live on patriotism alone; he lives on all the necessary conditions that enable him to ply his trade.

Expectedly, in Bantu Africa, to say nothing of the rest of Africa, the mass departure of the skilled manpower, the brain drain as it is now called, led to chronic poor service delivery and lack of industrial development due to technological incompetence. Hospitals, clinics, schools, colleges, universities and so forth went understaffed and millions of Bantu Africans failed to overcome ignorance and diseases. And without industrial development millions further stagnated into vending mushrooms and caterpillars, sweeping streets and cleaning gutters, chopping wood and burning charcoal, and tilling tired lands to their unending poverty. Industrial output in Bantu Africa foundered. Even simple commodities like soap, and sugar could hardly be manufactured. As a result a critical shortage of commodities became the order of the day. Every 1kg of sugar always had not less than 50 people jostling to buy it; and every tablet of soap, not less than 10. Ultimately this bred open mass discontent and disillusionment with nationalist governments. Weary of cheering their leaders driven in big Mercedes Benz cars while they lined the roads barefoot and with shabby clothes veiling their empty stomachs, they broke into food riots, strikes, and all sorts of civil strife agitating for change of leadership.

Within the very first term of nationalist leaders' suppressive rule, opposition leaders came up to answer to the people's call for new leadership. Educated men and women drawn from various professions that could not properly thrive and adequately contribute to the development of their countries due to suppression rose to challenge nationalist leaders' suppressive ideas. They argued for the right to own and enjoy the fruits of one's labour; they called for people to be at liberty to prosper. They pointed out that by suppressing the prosperity of their people, nationalist governments were not only denying their people the liberty which they and their forefathers pursued for hundreds of years as one of their fundamental liberation causes but also curtailing the development of their countries. Born out by great political and economic philosophers of all time such as John Locke and Adam Smith and many prosperous nations they inspired like the USA, Britain, and Japan, these new champions of African liberty asserted that professions, commerce, industry, farming—be it done by peasants or commercial farmers—and nations at large thrived if allowed to operate in an enabling liberal environment.

Now, if there is anything that brought the worst out of nationalist leaders and saw them compound their betrayal of the fundamental African liberation causes, it was challenging their ideas and authority. Like their predecessors, the African kings and emperors who never brooked challenges to their ideas and authority and purged challengers with banishments, enslavement and extermination, nationalist leaders developed a fierce aversion to criticism and critics. Driven by this aversion, they moved, with sheer brutality and manipulation, to smother liberty altogether in their countries just because it was liberty that enabled their people to object to their impoverishing ideas and point out alternative ones. They became totalitarian dictators and wiped out political opportunities of their challengers who, through their own opposition political parties were championing liberal ideas and alternative ways of successfully governing their countries, and thus deprived their people opportunities to ever elect themselves alternative governments which would redress their poverty. They brushed aside the objections of the majority of their people and declared their countries one-party states where everyone had to pledge loyalty to them, their ruling parties, and suppressive ideas. They abolished presidential electoral contests where they could be openly challenged by opposition leaders or anyone at all espousing alternative ways of governing their countries and from then on they alone contested the elections on a '*Yes or No*' ballot. And for all their people's open dissatisfaction with them, they always managed to record over 90% victories.

In Bantu Africa disputing such mysterious results or anything concerning governance was no longer permissible under the one-party rule. The press which was supposed to air or publish all such concerns were muzzled. Journalists stopped hearing and seeing evil. And those who persisted to want to discuss perceived evils in their countries with the press or other concerned citizens only had themselves to blame when the totalitarian law visited them and hurled them into death-jails. Unfortunately, throughout the late 1960s, all through the 1970s and 1980s death-jails claimed many lives of promising opposition Bantu African leaders in Malawi, Uganda, Kenya, Zaire (D.R. Congo) and Zambia who could not just shut up when their people and countries were clearly being impoverished and run down. Malawi's prominent opposition leader Orton Chirwa (1919 – 1992) died in jail while four of his colleagues were horrifically dispatched in an extra-judicial freak car accident; the trials and tribulations and, indeed, fate of several post-independence Ugandan opposition politicians, church leaders,

and professionals are now stuff for horror movies; Kenya's
nationalist leaders even went one beyond the common-place jailing
of its opposition leaders by seeing some them—Tom Mboya (1930
– 1969) among them—quickly snuffed by assassins; since the
brutal killing of Patrice Lumumba (1925 -1961) in custody,
Mobuto Sese Seko's junta in Zaire made jailing and killing
opposition politicians into a repertoire no uncommon as that of
Franco Makiadi's rumba hits; and in Zambia despite Kenneth
Kaunda's penchant to flourish his Christian beliefs in public just as
he made fetish of his extra-large white handkerchief which he
claimed to symbolise love and peace and which, ironically, he once
said he started carrying it *"whilst in prison during the struggle for
independence,"* he could not spare even his own childhood best
friend and his former vice-president turned formidable opposition
leader, Simon Kapwepwe, being hurled into his death-jails. John
Mwanakatwe in *End of Kaunda Era* lamented the demise of Simon
Kapwepwe and that of Nalumino Mundia (1927 – 1988), another
of Zambia's illustrious opposition politicians who perished under
Kaunda's totalitarian tyranny:

*Kapwepwe and Mundia were arrested because they became
Kaunda's political opponents....*

*Kapwepwe was not treated well in detention although he had
at one time occupied high office as vice-President of the Republic.
Many of his UPP members, who were detained with him ... were
subjected to severe physical torture. Their physical strength and
wellbeing was impaired after release because of the severity of
their torture and ill-treatment in prison during detention.*

Failed and impoverished, stripped of liberty and robbed of

alternative leaders and ideas, for about three decades of independence under nationalist leaders, Bantu Africans went nowhere near realising their fundamental liberation causes. Any attempts to come out of the millennium deprivation gulf (MDG) in which they were flung and *marooned* by Europeans with their slave-trade and colonialism were obliterated. Self-rule drew a blank. It only benefitted Mobutu Sese Seko (1930 – 1997), Kenneth Kaunda, Kamuzu Banda (1898 – 1997), Idi Amin (c.1925 – 2003), Robert Mugabe, name them, and, of course, their families and circles of friends and leeches.

The most profound mistake in Bantu Africa's political history is for Bantu Africans to have ever subordinated their liberation causes of a better peaceful life, liberty, and secured own lands and property to a mere incidental cause of self-rule. The cause of self-rule was purely collateral, a procedural digression which unfortunately side-tracked Bantu Africans completely. It should be remembered that long before Europeans came to Africa in the 15th century, Africans, and Bantu Africans in particular, were self-ruled and already in pursuit of their fundamental liberation causes. Just as under self-ruled, Bantu African nationalist leaders, Bantu Africans under their own kings and emperors suffered unbearable enormities—tyranny, dispossession, slave raids, massacres, and exterminations—which on one hand impelled them to pursue their liberation causes and on another exposed them to European subjugation. And when Europeans eventually took over control, they hardly altered the dynamics of Bantu Africans' pursuit of their liberation causes, but merely stood in the way of a brewing revolt. And with their own monstrous perversity they only helped to set it off. Expectedly they took the full force of it; but in the process they obstructed the Bantu African revolt from its intended targets, Bantu African tyrannical kings, emperors, and rulers, who escaped unscathed to re-emerge as Bantu African totalitarian dictators.

6

The Purge of Totalitarian Dictators,

The Economic Failures, and

The Ascendancy of Bantu African Oligarchies

What is Black Empowerment when it seems to benefit not the vast majority but an elite that tends to be recycled?

—Archbishop Desmond Tutu.

The tragedy Zambia faces is recycling the same politicians like Michael Sata, Alexander Chikwanda, and Daniel Munkombwe who have the same mentality and expect a different result.

—Hakainde Hichilema.

After three decades of totalitarian rule, from the 1960s up to the 1990s, Bantu Africans could no longer be lulled by self-rule, nor deluded by a hollow nationalism, nor cowed by murderous totalitarian regimes. They could no longer bear self-rule which translated into self-induced poverty; they could no longer be contented with a nationalism punctuated with acute food shortages, sky-rocketing prices of scarce mealie-meal, sugar, and soap, mass joblessness, pathetic service delivery, and dreadful hopelessness; and neither could they tolerate any longer governments which thrived on the suppression of their people's rights, aspirations and expectations. Students, workers, peasant farmers, church groups, trade unions, policemen, soldiers, and the general populace could not help but rise against totalitarian leaders. They assailed them with invasive riots, strikes, boycotts, armed rebellions, massively celebrated military coups, and unrelenting condemnation from the pulpits, in newsletters and newspapers, and at endless funerals of loved ones who needlessly died in violent food riots and of cholera, typhoid, malaria, and so forth.

Shrewd opposition leaders once more quickly rose to the occasion. They seized the mass indignation against totalitarian regimes, harnessed it to the long abandoned Bantu African liberation causes of liberty and better peaceful lives they adeptly revived and rebranded in trendy terms of the times—democracy, multiparty politics, liberalisation, privatisation, vibrant economy and so forth—and whipped up an overwhelming political movement. Like a storm this movement shook, tore, and swept away all that stood in its way, totalitarian dictators, their constitutions, governments, political parties, and impoverishing ideologies. It tossed totalitarian leaders into free and fair electoral contests against opposition leaders. And reflecting the magnitude of the indignation Bantu Africans felt towards them, they were severely routed at the polls.

In Zambia, Kenneth Kaunda, who only three years before in 1988 had won over 90% of the votes in his one-man Presidential elections, garnered a paltry 24% of the 1991 multi-candidate, presidential electoral vote. His number one opposition challenger and leader of the Movement for Multi-Party Democracy (MMD), Frederick Chiluba (1943 – 2011), grabbed the Presidency with over 70% of the national vote. And in neighbouring Zaire (D.R. Congo) where Mobutu Sese Seko refused to yield to this movement, he was flushed out by an equally rampaging popular rebellion led by Laurent-Desire Kabila (1939 – 2001).

Only Zimbabwe's President Robert Mugabe survived this movement but only by the skin of his teeth. At the eleventh hour he played his trump-card. He let many Zimbabwean Bantu African families speedily realise at least one of their fundamental liberation causes of owning their own lands with his Fast-track Resettlement Programme. It won him considerable support among Bantu Africans who for many years even after independence were crammed in poor communal lands. But still he sustained deep political and economic wounds. His Fast-track Resettlement Programme was at the expense of thousands of white commercial farmers, the descendants of Cecil Rhodes' Pioneers, who were forcibly evicted from their *'ancestral'* farms with little or no compensation. They vindictively rose against him by massively supporting his political rivals and successfully lobbying the European international community to cripple his government with devastating economic sanctions. The Zimbabwean economy crumbled and reduced Zimbabwean dollars to chaff. A basketful of Zimbabwean dollars were required for one to buy a mere loaf of bread or to exchange with either an American dollar, the British pound, or the euro. Zimbabweans, including his supporters, found this unbearable; for relief they voted for his main challenger and European-backed Morgan Tsvangirai (b. 1952) in the Presidential elections that followed in 2007. For the first time Robert Mugabe lost the Presidential elections to his challenger. But he wasn't out yet. Morgan Tsvangirai did not win outright; he fell short of the required 51% threshold. Thus it called for the second round of voting to really bring to an end Mugabe's then 27-year rule. Realising how possibly close that prospect was, Mugabe resorted to violence. He let his soldiers, policemen, and party cadres beat up, kidnap, and even kill Tsvangirai's supporters in the run-up to the second round of voting. Even Tsvangirai himself ended up badly beaten. Consequently he was forced out of the second round of the Presidential election as the atmosphere deteriorated to bloody mayhem. Mugabe claimed victory. But he was roundly condemned for his atrocious conduct not only by the European international community but even by his fellow Bantu African leaders in the Southern African Development Community (SADC). Using fresh threats of further debilitating political and economic sanctions, they all put pressure on him to at least share power with Tsvangirai. And he complied; he let Tsvangirai become Prime Minister in-charge of government while he retained the Presidency as head of state with executive powers.

In general as the 20th century was drawing to a close, totalitarian leaders had been purged. Bantu Africa entered the 21st century with new leaders who boasted a liberal political and economic outlook. With evangelical zeal, they, the champions of liberty now in power, effected the democratisation of their countries' institutions and the liberalisation of their economies— they piously took out their governments out of business saying 'government had no business in business' and privatised to private individuals all state owned companies, properties, assets, and so forth. And with the encouragement and guidance of established democracies and liberal economies of the world, they boldly razed totalitarian government institutions and command economy structures in their countries. They promulgated new laws which demanded regular free and fair elections, limited terms of office, transparency, checks and balances, accountability, separation of powers, private sector driven economies, free market economies, and so forth.

And with Bantu African governments practically and legally divorced from business, unfettered laissez-faire prevailed in Bantu Africa. The onus fell on individual Bantu Africans to buy and own the many privatised state-owned companies, industries, properties, and assets and freely venture into any business of their choice and prosper. But this is a people who had just emerged from the suppression and deprivation of totalitarian regimes with absolutely nothing to their names. They lived hand to mouth. With what would they buy and own their privatised state-owned mining firms, fertiliser and chemical plants, bicycle and car assembly plants, clothes and blanket factories, bus companies, airlines, hotels, banks, shops, et cetera? They could not even dare to walk into any bank to borrow the required money: banks demanded collateral which they couldn't have. They were officially and practically landless and their houses could not be officially recognised as collateral. Thus only those Bantu African individuals in positions of authority, established traders of Asian origin, and a privileged few Bantu Africans who had managed to amass wealth by hook or by crook while serving totalitarian regimes made the most of their countries' privatisation programmes.

Regrettably, and, indeed, compounding the dejection of the majority of poor Bantu Africans, Bantu Africa's liberal governments turned to total strangers to take up their countries' privatised companies which their people had no capacity to acquire. Instead of enabling their poor people to access capital and partake in their countries booming private economies and produce the goods and services and industrial activities which were visibly lacking, they embarked on worldwide crusades to woo foreign investors into their countries to do the business at almost no cost but their capital. They promised foreign investors little or no tax on their business ventures, speedy and easy acquisition of properties—business houses and lands—needed for their businesses, cheap Bantu African labour, and a ready provision of raw materials, and many other incentives. They earnestly preached this as "creating an enabling environment for foreign investors or investment."

And foreign investors duly swooped into Bantu Africa. They took up old state-owned business houses and warehouses and converted them into plush shopping malls which glutted with foreign apples, sweets, drinks, soaps, toilet paper, and many such items. They also put up new and bigger shopping malls on any available municipal land in the commercial districts of Bantu Africa. It was the scramble for Bantu Africa all over again—colonisation revisited and revised as *ecolonisation* (economic colonisation.) And the poor Bantu African masses inevitably reverted to their historical role: providers of cheap raw materials and labour to rich foreigners and a ready market for foreign junk. And at the end of the day foreign investors once more funnelled their cool profits into their rich countries while Bantu Africans fell back into their millennium deprivation gulf (MDG).

Yes, despite the liberty liberal governments afforded them to undertake all sorts of businesses and prosper, Bantu Africans foundered in poverty and failed to realise their fundamental cause of a better life simply because they had nothing—they had no means, they had no lands, no property, and no access to capital. Thus for them self-determination now coupled with liberty still rung hollow.

On 22 January, 1999, after eight years of a relentless privatisation drive and unbridled laissez-faire in Zambia, President Frederick Chiluba who succeeded the totalitarian Kenneth Kaunda memorably admitted (during an address to the 3rd session of Zambia's 8thNational Assembly) that his Movement for Multi-party Democracy (MMD) government had failed to get the huge majority of Zambians out of abject poverty. The BBC reported Chiluba's admission as *"a rare acknowledgement of failure."* The Post, Zambia's leading independent newspaper, on 27 January, 1999 lashed out in its editorial:

The high level of poverty in Zambia are of course a direct result of the ruling MMD's myopic adoption of policies whose implications it never really understood—it was simply a matter of following fashion—the world trends. And realism today dictates that Zambia abandons this fashion madness and acts in the best interests of the great majority of its people who constitute more than 80 per cent— a majority that today lives in abject poverty.

But that was easier said than could be done. The situation was already beyond rectification. The failure of liberal governments, right on the heels of the betrayal by nationalist or totalitarian governments, plunged Bantu Africa into a political and economic black hole. Nothing and nobody seemed able to ever redress Bantu Africa's poverty. Governments simply ran out of feasible plans to redress their people's abject poverty. And with nothing much for them to do about their people's seemingly intractable plight, they resigned themselves to chicanery and graft to at least enrich themselves, their families, and friends. Both Zambia's President Frederick Chiluba and Malawi's Bakili Muluzi (b. 1943) and a number of their respective government officials were arrested for graft upon leaving office.

And successive Bantu African governments themselves who made a meal of fighting graft and throwing their predecessors in jail for it, could not find anything viable to do to tackle their people's poverty. And to while their time in office they too turned to graft. But with hind sight, knowing how it fouled their predecessors' nests, they perfectly blended it into legitimate government procedure. Starting with the hallowed democracy itself which ought to bring the people's chosen leaders and parties into power, they compromised its institutions that ensure checks and balances, separation of powers, and transparency by buying off opposition members of parliament, journalists, and entire media houses and made them their deputy ministers, permanent secretaries, and government mouthpieces respectively. And when it came to elections, the basis of democracy, they disenfranchised their poverty-stricken people with a whole range of election gifts— packs of salt, sugar, mealie-meal, clothes, meat, small amounts of money, and all sorts of 'philanthropic' services. Lost to apathy following the failure of liberal governments right on the heels of the betrayal by nationalist governments, Bantu Africans, especially those in rural areas where poverty is more acute, no longer found their votes any more valuable than the instant election gifts they received from wealthy candidates. They either ended up voting for these 'kind' candidates or avoided voting altogether, denying other candidates votes, and in both ways benefitting the 'generous' ones. Thus the wealthier one was, the more likely he or she was to buy his way into power and thereby making power, like everything else in Bantu Africa, justice, lands, property, access to capital, education, and health, a preserve of the rich and powerful.

That is why no matter how many times, and there have been several times, political parties are changed in Bantu Africa, and more often on the explicit platform of change itself, the same old, rich, and powerful politicians turn up in successive governments, albeit under new political parties. Zambians, for instance, may appear to have been ruled, since their independence, by three different political parties—the United National Independence Party (UNIP), the Movement for Multi-party Democracy (MMD), and the Patriotic Front (PF)—but in actual fact the rulers in all these three different political parties are one and the same people who merely make political parties drape round them like cloaks—same people, different cloaks at different times and occasions. In 2011, 20 years after Kenneth Kaunda's totalitarian UNIP government had been ousted; Zambians went to the polls clamouring for change, especially in urban areas. They wanted to see changed their MMD government leaders who had led and failed them for 20 years with their liberal policies. A new political party, the PF, sounded more plausible to deliver that change. But the PF leaders who were in the forefront championing that change and eventually received overwhelming votes for it were the same old, rich, and powerful leaders who had led Zambia as UNIP leaders under Kaunda and as MMD leaders under Chiluba. Michael Sata who won the PF the Presidency was a long serving government official in Kenneth Kaunda's totalitarian UNIP government. On 28 October, 2011 Kenneth Kaunda, at the 50th Anniversary celebration for US Peace Corps in Lusaka, Zambia, even expressed his gratitude, in reference to Michael Sata's Presidency, that "one of [his] boys was President." And for all his vitriolic condemnation of the MMD and its failed liberal policies, Sata was also one of MMD's senior most politicians who crafted and propagated the policies it followed in its 20-year old reign. Among the many senior positions or portfolios he held in the liberal MMD government was that of MMD's Chief Executive, Secretary General, and a forceful chief propagator of the MMD policies for that matter—he did not hesitate to etch them down on the heads of political opponents with machetes; many MMD opponents were left scarred Rwanda-style by his MMD cadres; and this villainy he would let his cadres, now as PF cadres, perpetuate with near impunity even after becoming President.

Dr Guy Scott (b. 1944), Michael Sata's Vice-President, both in the PF and government was once MMD's agricultural minister who is remembered by many Zambians for leaving peasant farmers to the tender mercies of liberal agricultural policies. Himself being a land owning commercial farmer with lots of properties that gave him easy access to capital, he spearheaded MMD's unbridled liberalised agricultural policies which expected landless peasant farmers to finance their own agricultural endeavours. Zambia is Bantu Africa's potential bread basket with its vast arable land and the Zambian staple is locally grown white mealie-meal; but Dr Scott thus ended up running down Zambia's agricultural production to the point that he had Zambians unforgettably eat yellow mealie-meal which was donated to them as food aid by foreign governments and the United Nations.

President Sata's finance minister, Alexander Chikwanda, and most probably his real vice-President as he is the one who acts as President whenever he is out instead of Guy Scott all because he is white (his parents came from Scotland in 1927), was equally Kenneth Kaunda's finance minister in 1971, 42 years before. And several of President Sata's cabinet ministers, Sylvia Masebo, Nkandu Luo, and Wynter Kabimba, and many deputy ministers were MMD cabinet ministers, deputy ministers, and party officials. Effectively setting up an oligarchy in Zambia, President Sata's entire PF government was made up of former top UNIP and MMD leaders whose respective totalitarian and liberal policies betrayed and failed Zambians as we have already seen. And apart from bringing back into government former UNIP and MMD leaders,

President Sata reinstated many former directors and chief executives of government departments who had been either fired or retired by the UNIP and MMD governments. His government even controversially proposed and advocated that the retirement age in Zambia be moved from 55 years to 65 years to accommodate these retired directors, judges, and chief executives.

Asked by Zambia's Post Newspapers in April 2013 what he was still doing in government at 81 years of age, one of President Sata's old, rich and powerful ministers, outspoken 81-year old Daniel Munkombwe, who saw himself in all three of Zambia's governments since independence, let the cat out of the bag. He blurted out that he and his colleagues had a penchant to be always in government purely as a self-seeking venture:

There is nobody who is not using my philosophy of politics of benefitting oneself. There is nobody who goes into parliament naked; we go to parliament because of allowance. There is no more patriotism. Patriotism was only there when we were fighting colonialists, so everybody is adapting my philosophy of politics of benefits. [And all this for a governing party calling itself the Patriotic Front.] I know people will say Munkombwe has gone into government because he wants to eat but who doesn't want to eat?

If the PF, despite being essentially made up of the same old, rich and powerful politicians who had always been at the helm of Zambian politics and government, had made a difference in people's lives, if they had changed the plight of Zambians, if they had redressed the abject poverty afflicting the majority of Zambians, their coming to power under this new party would have been justified. But as it can be deduced from Munkombwe's sentiments above, nothing else really changed.

The jobs they promised the youths during the election campaign were mostly given to their retired peers, family members, friends, and staunch party cadres with or without qualifications and, interestingly, when asked where the jobs he promised the ordinary masses were, President Sata fell to citing our proverbial construction and maintenance of roads, slashing of grass along the roads, cleaning gutters, and sweeping the streets as "*thousands and thousands of jobs*" he and his government had created; and the "*more money*" in the pockets of Zambians he and his party promised actually ended up in the pockets of their family members, friends, and staunch party cadres they employed in the civil service only to embezzle with impunity huge amounts of money meant for public service works (and this is according to the Zambian Auditor General's reports) and, indeed, themselves as they increased their salaries more than a hundredfold immediately they formed the PF government. President Sata's basic salary per annum which he had increased three times in only two years of the PF's rule moved from K164, 000 ($ 30, 000), which his immediate predecessor, President Rupiah Banda was receiving in 2011, to K 414, 406 ($80, 000) by October 2013. Likewise the basic salaries per annum of his Vice President, Cabinet Ministers, deputy ministers, Members of Parliament, Permanent Secretaries, diplomats, and all constitutional office holders respectively trebled in just 2 years of the PF's government. By contrast, the peasant farmer who constitutes 80% of Zambia's population and who produces over 90% of Zambia's staple food, still received K65 ($ 13) for his 50kg bag of maize, the same price he received in 2011 when the MMD and Rupiah Banda were in government.

In essence the changes that occurred had no bearing on the plight of the huge majority of Zambians. Changing the name of Lusaka International Airport to Kenneth Kaunda Airport;

Livingstone International Airport, to Harry Mwaanga Nkhumbula Airport; Ndola International Airport, to Simon Mwansa Kapwepwe; Ndola Stadium, to Levy Mwanawasa Stadium—which President Sata announced without even having some of these institutions refurbished, did not alleviate the suffering of the vast majorities of Zambians in any way. Neither did declaring every remote Zambian settlement a district, which President Sata relished doing especially during each and every by-election campaign as a ploy to woo voters to vote for the PF, when in reality his government had no capacity and resources to fund and develop these settlements into functional districts.

Crucially, nothing too came of President Sata's self-diagnosed and much publicised *"allergy to corruption"* which he pronounced upon assuming the Presidency. Without doubt seriously tackling corruption which has infected every sector of Zambia's economy, civil service, and government would have provided many unemployed and poverty-stricken Zambians proper productive jobs, business opportunities, medical attention, education places, and poverty alleviation projects they deserve. But day in and day out opportunities for better jobs, businesses, healthcare, education, and government support still favour those with party, family, and financial connections and not merit. Even President Levy Mwanawasa's and President Rupiah Banda's Farm Input Support Programme (FISP) and Food Reserve Agency (FRA) crop markets which were designed to uplift the lives of many poor peasant farmers in Zambia, became completely gutted by graft and blatant thefts by government officials and the rich. The vast majorities of poverty-stricken peasant farmers were left underserviced or completely cut out. Government officials and the rich recruited hordes of poor peasants themselves to receive FISP farm inputs and sell crops to the FRA on their behalf. While the hordes of poor peasants walked home with a few Kwachas only which could not even buy them their own bag of fertiliser, government officials and the rich ended up with loads of wealth—mansions, fleets of cars, buses, and trucks.

Most probably President Sata became *"allergic to corruption,"* at such a an advanced age, he was 75 years old when he made the self-diagnosis, that it could not in any way affect his conduct and way of governing he had grown accustomed to. In 1994 Levy Mwanawasa, Zambia's real anti-graft crusader, gave up the republican vice-presidency and the privileges it underpinned on account of being nauseated by no other than Michael Sata's corrupt practices as an MMD minister which their boss, President Frederick Chiluba, seemed to condone due to his failure to take action against Sata in spite of several reports. And emulating how President Chiluba tolerated his reported corrupt practices, rather than paying heed to his late-life self-diagnosed *"allergy to corruption,"* President Sata, without any squeamish at all, readily ignored reports by the media and some of his cabinet ministers that two of his ministers, the PF Secretary General and Justice Minister, Wynter Kabimba, and Defence Minister, Geoffrey Mwamba, were involved in serious corrupt practices; in fact, he instead scolded Zambia's Anti-Corruption Commission (ACC) for duly instituting investigations against the two allegedly corrupt ministers without his approval.

Corruption is now the bane of Bantu Africans' existence; but it is, paradoxically, the lifeline of Bantu Africa's oligarchies. In most Bantu African countries it is said that democracy is blighted by tribal politics. It is perceived that most politicians are elected into office out of tribal loyalty and not their political acumen or merits. But ethnic tribalism is only a thin veneer of one really domineering and democracy threatening tribe in Bantu Africa: the rich and powerful that form Bantu Africa's oligarchies whose lifeline is corruption. Bantu Africa's rich and powerful now constitute a long time domineering tribe which but comes from all Bantu Africa's ethnic tribes. Although numerically small, it is less than 10%of the entire Bantu African population, it has a paralysing ascendancy. Like a spider it spins its lifeline, corruption, over democracy, government, business, the civil service, and every facet of Bantu African national life and eventually gut them.

Adeptly, Bantu African oligarchies play the ethnic tribal card, among their many deceptive ploys, to woo the unsuspecting ordinary Bantu African who still believes in his or her ethnic tribe's supremacy to vote for them. But once voted into power they have little in common with their ethnic tribesmen but a lot with fellow parliamentarians and ministers from various neglected ethnic tribes. Among their fellow MPs and ministers they will award themselves hefty salaries, allowances and gratuities while their ethnic tribesmen walk in rags and feed on maize bran. Throughout their stay in power they will preoccupy themselves with playing golf, dancing and dining together and laughing merrily at their good life and never spare a thought, let alone a moment, for the suffering of their ethnic tribesmen.

Statics are bound of Presidents, vice-Presidents, ministers, and MPs in Bantu Africa whose village communities live in abject poverty. Yet the same Presidents, Vice-Presidents, ministers, and MPs have considerably assisted their friends across the ethnic tribal divide, and even racial divide, that they and their children will never know poverty. For a cut a Chewa President gives a lucrative contract to a Bemba or Indian colleague. And this continues back and forth among Bantu Africa's oligarchies that they perpetuate themselves in power to the detriment or deprivation of the vast majorities of their ethnic tribesmen who are reduced to dregs of their society.

And, as we have already seen above, all this rot in Bantu Africa now stems from that same failure by Bantu African leaders to redress their people's chronic poverty, to rescue Bantu Africans from the millennium deprivation gulf (MDG). Corruption or graft is only a malignant tumour that grows in place of effective and pragmatic solutions to a people's poverty

7

Land

Nobody ever dreams of giving the poor a chance to help themselves....

You can only cure affects by curing the cause. Every sin and every wrong that exists in the world is the product of law, and you cannot cure it without curing the cause....

Without Land man cannot live; without access to it man cannot labour.

—Clarence Darrow.

If history could teach us anything, it would be that private property is inextricably linked with civilisation.

—Ludwig von Mises.

Property is the Pivot of civilisation.

—Leon Samson.

Most of the loans we have issued have been salary-based, but title deeds will give more Zambians access to bank loans and a means to partner with foreign investors who are looking for land or property where they can set up businesses without any wrangles over who owns the property.

—Reginald Mubanga, Stanbic Bank Zambia Limited.

In any people's existence land is a bedrock of all economics, a springboard to prosperity, and a treasure-trove of all wealth. Bantu Africa's own troubled history has comprehensively demonstrated this. Cecil Rhodes, as already seen in the previous chapters, ensured that his white settler communities in Bantu Africa set up viable economies and prospered by letting them freely own and utilise Bantu African lands. The same is true of all white settlers in Bantu Africa: in South Africa, Namibia, Kenya, Malawi, and so forth European settlers have founded their abiding affluence on Bantu African lands they own and exploit. Even for modern day European investors and, indeed, any other foreign investors, be they Chinese, Indian, American, and so forth, Bantu African governments woo into their countries, securing and owning Bantu African lands is a prerequisite to all their economic endeavours in Bantu Africa. In 1998, at the height of Zambia's quest to woo foreign investors in the country, the then Director General of Zambia Investment Centre, Margret Mwanakatwe, told a group of Germany businessmen who were touring Zambia that: *"Once we grant you an investment licence, it will be our obligation to help you secure title deeds as soon as possible, because it is our interest, your interest and that of the larger Zambian economy that you get started as soon as possible."*

But Bantu Africans themselves have been systematically and openly barred to own their lands for hundreds of years now. No Bantu African ruler or government has ever felt obliged to help its people "secure title deeds as soon as possible." (According to the ministry of Lands and natural resources in Zambia only 80 thousand people out of Zambia's 14 million people have title deeds to their lands and property.) Perhaps it is not in their people's interest, and their own interest, and that of the large Bantu African economy that they "get started as soon as possible." Thus the lot of landless Bantu Africans, who make about 90% of Bantu Africa's 500 million people, is intractable want and deprivation.

In all sincerity, as long as the huge majority of Bantu Africans are landless, so long will be their impoverishment, destitution, and want. No Bantu African government will ever succeed to better the lot of its people without ensuring that individually or as individual families they are granted titled lands, land in which their houses, shops, boreholes, wells, fruit trees, and timber will become real assets and indispensable collateral; lands which they can individually lease out and raise money for other economic ventures such as processing their produce or buying shares in manufacturing companies; and lands which they can, indeed, freely sell and use the money to start new businesses and new lives altogether other than peasantry.

As the world's population increasingly gets bigger, vast tracts of lands are badly needed in which to grow crops to feed it. And the production of such crops to feed the world's 8 billion people is no longer a peasant farmer's business with his pristine hoe and axe; it is now a multi-trillion dollar undertaking for multi-national companies with their array of high-tech equipment, fertilisers, chemicals, genetically modified seeds, and bags of money. But distinctly missing in that array of their agricultural might are arable lands. They have run out of arable lands in their homelands— Europe, Asia, and the Americas—in which to carry out their extensive multi-trillion dollar farming. They are right now busy searching and acquiring arable lands far away from their homelands. In Bantu Africa too they have arrived. A BBC Focus on Africa Magazine reporter, John Hogg, in 2010 hailed their arrival in Africa as *"A brilliant development opportunity."* But he quickly paralleled the phenomenon to colonisation and expressed his apprehension that yet again it was being perpetrated at the expense of Bantu Africans. In his article titled, 'On Shaky Ground,' which appeared in the BBC Focus on Africa Magazine of January-March 2010, he wrote: *"A brilliant development opportunity or yet another attempt by neo-colonialists to harness Africa's potential? This new battle ground is land and some African countries have already surrendered."*

Unfortunate as Bantu Africans are, that surrender by their countries only means one thing: another of their blessings, after their race, gold, diamonds, and oil, is turning out to be a curse. Instead of reaping a windfall over their lands by selling or leasing them out to the voracious agribusiness land investors, they stand to lose out completely. For want of title deeds to their lands they have inhabited for hundreds of years, their governments and chiefs are instead selling their lands, pocketing the billions of dollars thus made, and driving them out with absolutely nothing. John Hogg in his article, 'On Shaky Ground,' seen above, concedes that *"The land-owning rights of Africans are weak which means it is easy for governments to parcel up and hand out territory to foreign investors."* So the spectre of dispossession is once more looming large in all of Africa.

That 50 years after the end of the European subjugation of Bantu Africans the majority of them can't lay claim even to minute pieces of lands where their houses stand, that 50 years after independence the property of the majority of Bantu Africans is officially null and void because it stands on lands which officially do not belong to them although it is their motherland and ancestral land, that 50 years after attaining self-rule Bantu Africans are still, in the famous words of the South African author and ANC's first Secretary General, Sol Plaatje (1876 – 1932), *"Pariahs in the land of their birth,"* that half a century after Europeans left Bantu Africans to shape their own destiny they still can't actualise such a life-changing prospect as making good with their lands for want of title deeds, when, as a matter of fact, land security and ownership was one of the three fundamental Bantu African liberation causes, Bantu Africans were short-changed by their leaders at independence. Immediately after independence Bantu African leaders ought to have embarked on deliberate universal land dispensation programmes that would have allowed Bantu Africans to own their lands—just as Cecil Rhodes did for his settlers immediately they took over Matabeleland and Mashonaland or as Robert Mugabe belatedly and controversially did with his Fast-track Land Resettlement Programme—not only as a reward for their contribution to liberating their own lands from foreign occupation but also as their rightful inheritance and a springboard to their economic life. On 25 February, 2004 Theo-Ben Gurirab, the Prime Minister of Namibia, where, remember, the Herero and Nama Bantu African people were almost exterminated by the Germans over their lands, tried to disarmingly absorb the charge of short-changing their people over their lands. He told Namibia's national Radio and TV that, *"The problem of land ownership was indeed central to the struggle for national independence. Today, generations after the systematic dispossession, our young nation still struggles to bring about balance and undo the effects of the unjust land distribution."*

Admittedly, it's quite a complicated process to reclaim lands from people who have developed them for a long time and return them to their supposed rightful owners. The convulsions and upheavals that recently characterised Robert Mugabe's Fast-track Land Resettlement Programmes are typical of the process. Otherwise to avoid repaying a wrong with a wrong, dispossession with dispossession, huge financial implications have to be taken into consideration to possibly compensate those affected by the programme. But what is wicked and totally inexcusable of any Bantu African government is the fact that they still cannot easily let the majority of their people own even the indisputable minute pieces of lands where their very houses and gardens stand, so much so that those houses and gardens are of little economic value. What difficulty is there in granting the majority of their people title deeds to their homelands other than lack of political *will, culpable* negligence, and deliberate Bantu African state policies to perpetuate the "systematic dispossession" of their people? It must suit Bantu African governments and chiefs, as it did Bantu African kings and emperors and later colonial authorities, that Bantu Africans have no legal claim to their lands and property therein as it makes it easy for them to simply demolish their structures, drive them into some remote and poor locality, and sell their lands to wealthy land developers.

In June 2004 the New African, an illustrious Africanist magazine, let one of its book reviewers, Osei Boateng, trash a book entitled *The Shackled Continent—Africa's Past, Present, and Future*, written by Robert Guest, the then Africa editor of The Economist. Boateng wrote of Guest's book: *"This is the kind of book you read holding your nose, so those who do not have handkerchiefs, please go to the nearest shop and get yourself one."* What incurred *The Shackled Continent* and Robert Guest that contempt was his audacity, being white, to bluntly point out in it some shocking but not so well concealed deformities afflicting the majority of Africans. Robert Guest stated in *The Shackled Continent*—Africa's Past, Present, and Future that, *"Most Africans do not own their own homes."* He also conceded that most of them, over 80% of all Africans, live in rural areas. To which Osei Boateng reacted:

So who owns the homes in the rural areas? The government? Apparently, to him, African 'homes' do not count as homes because they are built with 'mud and sticks'.

Quite very so and not quite so at all, Mr Boateng. Implausible and ridiculous as it sounds, Bantu African governments and, by extension, chiefs do really own their people's homes in so far as they own the lands wherever those homes stand. And 80% to 90% of Bantu African homes be it in rural areas or urban shanty compounds *"do not count as homes"* not necessarily because they are built with *"mud and sticks"* and cardboard and plastics but because they are virtually squatter structures whose owners Bantu

African governments and chiefs never recognise with proper title deeds which banks, business houses, courts of law, and indeed other people such as Robert Guest and his compatriots, who properly "own their own homes" with right documents, can honour and respect.

The ignominy of being huddled in a Bantu African village or shanty compound where houses of individuals are never officially recognised as their assets or property is similar to being buried in a mass grave. No wonder the term '*villager*' in Bantu Africa is loaded with derogatory connotations. A villager is synonymous with a nonentity, a worthless person, a scum of the earth. And the misfortune of living in an untitled own house is equivalent to being buried in an unmarked grave. While in a mass grave one's remains will be lost in a pile of indistinguishable bones; in an unmarked grave they will be lost among many an unrecognisable grave. We cannot, therefore, blame anyone for pointing out such obnoxious realities which endlessly shackle Bantu Africa's landless majorities.

To free themselves from their proverbial mindless toil and destitution, to transcend their proverbial role of being miserable choppers of wood, tappers of rubber-trees, and growers of cotton and grain, to rescue themselves out of the millennium deprivation gulf (MDG), Bantu Africans have no option but to process their wood, sap, grain, cotton, and even minerals. They have to industrialise both their production of basic raw materials and the manufacture of end products if they are to thrive and prosper like the Europeans, the Americans, and the Asians. The vast markets of the modern world crave for paper and furniture and not wood; denims and linen, and not lint and flax; shoes and jackets, and not hides and sap. Industrialisation is now the lingua franca of modern commerce and trade; those fluent in it prosper tremendously. And no world market ever understands and has time to respect and treat fairly Bantu Africa's logs, barrels of sap, metric tons of hides, copper, cocoa, cotton, and many such raw produce.

In The *Shackled Continent—Africa's Past, Present, and Future*, Robert Guest again assiduously points all this out:

Countries grow wealthy in much the same way that individuals do: by making things that other people want to buy or providing services that others will pay for…. By and large, the route to prosperity is through thrift, hard work, and finding out what other people want in order to sell it to them. Britain first grew rich, in the 19th century, by using newly invented industrial techniques to produce cheaper and better textiles, steel, railways, and other goods, which both locals and foreigners were kin to buy.

Japan grew rich in the 20th century by adapting and improving manufacturing techniques invented elsewhere, in order to make better and cheaper cars, semiconductors, and fax machines. America is the world's richest country today because so many people crave American movies, medicines, aeroplanes, and banking services.

Africa, in contrast, hardly produces anything that the rest of the world wants to buy…

And this again unfortunately earned Robert Guest a totally unwarranted lampoon from Osei Boateng. In the same New African book review of June 2004, Boateng scoffed:

This indeed is hilarious stuff! "Africa is poor because it hardly produces anything that the rest of the world wants to buy?"

Really? And this coming from the African editor of the Economist?
So, who buys all those gold, diamonds, uranium, copper, cocoa,
coffee, tea, and the thousands of other minerals that Africa
produces? Africans themselves?

Osei Boateng was, again, way wide of the mark. Africa's
export of raw "*gold, uranium, copper, cocoa, coffee, tea, and the*
thousands of other minerals that it produces" was precisely what
Robert Guest deplored and held responsible for its
underdevelopment. And, indeed, seven years later Boateng himself
came full circle and fervently embraced this point. In an April
2011 issue of the New African magazine particularly dedicated to
his feature, 'Cracking the Code—Unlocking Africa's Secret to
Wealth,' which unreservedly acknowledged Guest's point without,
astonishingly, mentioning him and his book at all but instead
abundantly hailing as his feature's "star economists" Erik S.
Reinert (b. 1949) for his book, *How Rich Countries Got Rich...and*
Why Poor Countries Stay Poor, published in English in 2007, and
Ha-Joon Chang (b. 1963) for his book, *Bad Samaritans—The*
Guilty Secrets of Rich Nations & the Threat to Global Prosperity,
also published in 2007, Boateng warned:

History shows that no country has ever become rich by exporting
foodstuffs and raw materials without also having an industrial
sector and in modern terms, an advanced service sector. The more
a country specialises in the production of raw materials, the
poorer it becomes. But this is a lesson Africa has still not learned.

Well conceded, save it is never really out of ignorance that Africans, especially Bantu Africans, are still miserable exporters of *"food stuffs and raw materials."* Bantu Africans already know too well that it is imperative for them to industrialise, to process their produce, if they are to create themselves decent rewarding jobs and prosper. This is one of the commonest elementary knowledge which almost every Bantu African is aware of even without going to school. But the problem is that they simply have no capacity and means to industrialise. Industrialisation does not come cheap. It calls for huge capital investment in technology and machinery. And throughout the world entrepreneurs, investors, and industrialists raise capital on capital markets with their assets. But Bantu Africans, on the contrary, cannot lay claim even to their assets. They are still systematically deprived of their assets. Legally they are not permitted to use their untitled houses to secure loans from lending institutions, nor lease their lands, nor entirely sell both their lands and houses to establish food processing and clothes manufacturing plants and earn themselves fulfilling jobs and prosperous lives.

Zambia's President Michael Sata, an accomplished simulation tactician, once expressed synthetic remorse for helplessly presiding over Zambians who, like the rest of Bantu Africans, suffer systematic deprivation. Addressing international delegates on 21June 2012 at the Rio + 20 World Conference on climate change and sustainable development in Brazil, Mr Sata said:

Zambia has only 13 million people, which is the population of some of the cities in the world. But out of those 13 million, it is most unfortunate that a lot of people are unemployed and God will never forgive us for that.

This is so because we have not managed and used our natural

resources [such as lands] the way we are supposed to use them,
for the benefit of our people.

But many progressive leaders throughout the world who
genuinely felt for their people in a similar predicament did not wait
for God to have a say over the matter. They straight away led their
people into historic revolutions that overthrew the systems that
impoverished them, revolutions that granted them land ownership
and security and set in motion breathtaking feats of
industrialisation and economic advancement that completely
altered their destiny. 50 years ago, when Bantu Africans were
reclaiming their autonomy, the Shah of Iran, Mohammad Reza
Pahlavi (1919 – 1980) accomplished the "White Revolution" for
Iranians in 1963. According to the Wikipedia the "White
Revolution made it possible for 1.5 million peasant families, who
had once been little more than slaves, to own the lands that [like
Bantu Africans] they had been cultivating all their lives." The
White Revolution, the granting of land ownership to millions of
Iranians, and not Iran's undisputed oil wealth, subsequently
transformed Iran into a modern Industrial country that it is today.
In his 1982 history book, *World History in the Twentieth Century*,
R.D. Cornwell substantiates:

Despite the importance of oil in Iran, agriculture was the real
basis of the economy, with three-quarters of the population
dependant on farming.... Land was owned by a relatively small
number of land lords before 1962. The peasants, who lived near
subsistence level with no prospect of improving their lot, provided
labour and were not far removed from serfdom... [But] in 1962 the
redistribution of land, [which] in effect...was a social revolution,
for the power of old landowners was broken and a large number of

small peasant landowners was created....

These agricultural changes ensured that during the twenty-five years between 1953 and 1978 [of the Shah's reign] the standard of living of the mass of Iranians rose.

Prior to the 2013 summit of the world's leading emerging economies and newly industrialised countries of the BRICS (Brazil, Russia, India, China, and South Africa) held in South Africa, President Jacob Zuma (b. 1942) of South Africa hosted President Xi Jinping (b. 1953) of China and said: *"We view China's success as a source of hope and inspiration as we engage with the task of finding our own solutions for bringing about a better future.... The rise of China therefore has lessons for us all as we seek to emulate your example."*

But Bantu Africa's favourite model economy and most intimate trade and development partner, China (80% of Bantu Africa's raw minerals feed China's rapid industrialisation), has as well painstakingly inscribed much of those *'lessons'* on its own land. China owes its emergence as a viable modern nation, as the now mighty People's Republic of China, to the painful endeavours of its masses to own their lands. Although the huge majority of China's 1.5 billion people still do not explicitly own the lands they inhabit in China, they and their forefathers traced out the political and economic frontiers of modern China with their enduring and really illustrative 'long march' to land ownership.

In October, 2007 I went to China to attend a month-long agricultural and economic development seminar at Zhejiang University which the sponsors, the Chinese Ministry of Commerce, dubbed *"Small Farmers Adapting to the Global Markets."* In his paper entitled 'China's Land (re)Distribution and Economic

Development' presented to 60plus international delegates of us drawn from over 30 countries from South America, Asia, Asia Pacific, Europe, the Middle East, and Africa, Professor Xiaopeng Luo, who was guest Professor at Zhejiang University from 2006 to 2010, disclosed that historically in China "*Land was the most legitimate asset, much more so than financial or other capital.*" As a result, the purchase of property in land... became the most important source of superior social status and economic insurance." Therefore, during the Qing dynasty (1616 – 1911) much of the land in China was acquired by very few wealthy people. The masses, mostly peasants, were reduced to mere squatters who were made to pay huge taxes and rents to these few wealthy landlords for cultivating and living on the lands.

Thus after the 1911 Chinese Revolution that overthrew the Qing dynasty, the founding father of modern China, Dr Sun Yat-Sen (1866 – 1925), set out to establish a modern Republic of China with his Kuomintang (the Nationalist People's Party) he formed in 1912 based on three objectives or the "*Three Principles of the People,*" as Dr Yat-Sen himself and the Kuomintang called them. These were nationalism, democracy, and land reform (much more like Bantu Africa's own three fundamental liberation causes of autonomy, liberty, and secured own lands). Dr Yat-Sen wanted the modern Republic of China to be free from European and Japanese imperialism which was the order of the day before and even after the 1911 Chinese Revolution. And himself having gone to school in a democratic world, USA's Hawaii and Britain's Hong Kong, he wanted this autonomous new republic of China to be united and people-driven as opposed to the warlords who carved up China after the 1911 revolution. And then, not least in any way, he strongly believed that the Chinese masses who throughout China lived in poverty, impoverished by a few wealthy landlords who charged them huge amounts of money as taxes and rents for use of the land, could attain themselves a better livelihood if land was fairy redistributed and made to be owned by individual peasants. These objectives, especially that of wanting to radically reform the land policy in China won the Kuomintang considerable support from the Chinese masses. Even nascent Communist disciples such as the then young Mao Zedong chose to fall under the umbrella and leadership of Dr Sun Yat-Sen's Kuomintang.

But after assuming both political and military control of all China in 1927 with such massive support of the Chinese masses who hoped for the promised radical land reforms to materialise so that they could own their own lands, the new Kuomintang leader, General Chiang Kai-Shek, who succeeded Dr Sun Yat-Sen upon his death in 1925, aligned himself with wealthy landlords and reneged on affecting land reforms. R.D.Cornwell in his history book, *World History in the Twentieth Century*, writes: *"Chiang could claim to have achieved Sun's first principle, nationalism, but relying as he did on the support of wealthy land owners, no moves were made towards democracy or land reform...."*

However, fearing a possible backlash from the deeply disappointed landless masses and Communists who were passionate about breaking the few wealthy landlord's control of much of Chinese lands, General Chiang Kai-Shek, encouraged and supported by the wealthy landlords, embarked on a ruthless campaign to purge Communists and peasant activists in the Kuomintang and throughout China. Thousands of Communists and peasants were massacred in cold blood in what became known as the Shanghai Massacre of 1927. Norman Lowe in his own history book, *Mastering Modern World History*, says *"Some estimates put the total murdered [in this massacre] as high as 250, 000."*

Young Mao Zedong and a group of fellow lucky Communists managed to escape to Jiangxi province in South-East China. There, with renewed promises of reclaiming land from the wealthy landlords and the Kuomintang and redistribute it to the landless peasants, Mao and his group of Communists managed to mobilise thousands of landless peasants into a peasant militia poised to not only topple the Kuomintang government but to instantly reclaim and redistribute the land wherever their forces were in control. But before Mao Zedong and his peasant militia could take the war to the Kuomintang, General Chiang Kai-Shek's Kuomintang forces followed and surrounded them in South-East China in 1937. They, the peasants and Communists, were again massacred in large numbers before Mao Zedong and a contingent of 86, 000 peasant militia and Communists again managed to audaciously rescue themselves and flee over 10,000 km of difficult terrain to North-West China and thereby accomplish the legendary *"Long March."*

Out of the 86, 000 Communist and peasant militia who broke out of the Kuomintang encirclement in Jiangxi, only about 9, 000 completed the Long March and reached their new place of refuge in Yunan, Northern China. It was with these and from Yunan that Mao Zedong revived his political and military campaign against the Kuomintang. Again using promises of instant land acquisition from the despised wealthy landlords and redistribution to the poor landless masses, he rapidly rallied millions of landless peasants throughout the countryside to his cause. In reference to Mao Zedong's use of land acquisition and redistribution to muster this groundswell of landless peasant support, Professor Luo in his paper, 'China's Land (re)Distribution and Economic Development,' attests that:

Through radical land reform, revolutionaries could redistribute the land of absentee landlords..., as well as those controlled by local outlaws, to needy peasants and establish revolutionary regimes with their support. Mao Zedong successfully used this opportunity to achieve a revolutionary strategy of the countryside surrounding the towns....

Radical land reform was again to become a powerful means of regime change in China. The poor peasants, who gained land, actively participated in the People's Liberation Army, becoming a decisive factor in the civil war won by the CCP [the Chinese Communist Party.]

But again after assuming total control of China, having driven General Kai-Shek and the Kuomintang and over 2 million wealthy landlords out of mainland China onto the island of Taiwan and, consequently, proclaiming mainland China the People's Republic of China in 1949—Mao Zedong and the victorious Communist Party of China equally faltered. They found the prospect of really granting land ownership to millions and millions of their individual peasants, who bravely helped to rid China of the Kuomintang and the greedy wealthy landlords with that precise aspiration, incompatible with their Communist ideology. For them letting their masses realise their aspiration of owning their own lands was politically subversive, flirting with one of capitalism's cardinal sins: private ownership of property, which they had just painstakingly eradicated out of China with the expulsion of the Kuomintang and millions of their wealthy landowners. Mao Zedong in particular, despite himself being a son of landless peasants, was a bigoted Communist who could not countenance any form of private ownership of property be it that of wealthy landlords or that of landless peasants; he was devoted to all the precepts of Communism. And, on top this, he was determined to faithfully follow the example set by neighbouring big brother, Russia, who not only gave him tremendous support in his political and military campaign against the Kuomintang but had also travelled a similar path to establish the first Communist government in the world some 30 years before China.

Indeed, like Mao Zedong's Communists in China, Vladimir

Lenin's Communists in Russia, the Bolsheviks, rode on the backs of land seeking Russian peasants to assume power. While Lenin and fellow elite Communists were in exile (Lenin was in Switzerland) plotting an elaborate Communist revolution they wished to take place in Russia, the Russian peasants on their own staged the February 1917 Peasant Revolution in Russia that seized lands and property from aristocratic landowners in order to realise their own long held aspiration to own lands and property. 9 months later, in November 1917, Vladimir Lenin's Bolsheviks swopped in and hijacked this revolution. They superseded it with their own Communist revolution and government which not only frowned on the peasants' aspirations to own their lands but passed an infamous "Decree on Land" that totally banished all such aspirations in communist Russia. It said:

There could be no private ownership of land [in Russia.]

Land could not be sold, leased or mortgaged.

All privately owned land was to be confiscated by the government with no compensation paid.

Lenin's successor, Joseph Stalin, who viewed the prosperity of Russian peasants, the Kulaks as they were called in Russia, as a threat not only to Communism but also to his own authority fiercely, upheld this decree. Using it as a weapon to suppress the prosperity of the kulaks rather than to uplift their standard of living, he ordered his Red Army to forcibly confiscate whatever lands and property which were in their individual names and then cram millions of them into collective state farms like prisoners. Any resistance to this vile collectivisation by the dispossessed kulaks was severely punished by death. Tens of millions of Kulaks were in the process impoverished and murdered. Impenitently Stalin memorably told his Red Army and Communist faithful that, *"We must smash the kulaks so hard that they will never rise to their feet again."*

This then is the Communism, complete with loss of millions and millions of innocent poor people's lives, Mao Zedong bigotedly tried to emulate in China with similar tragic results. Like Stalin, Mao systematically dispossessed the peasants of their produce and lands they may have acquired during the ousting of the Kuomintang and wealthy landlords. Professor Luo puts it mildly that, *"Prior to losing their land, China's peasantry lost the freedom to sell their agricultural products."* Mao, with his own version of collectivisation, which he called the *"People's Communes,"* and introduced with great exaltation as the *"Great Leap Forward,"* had multitudes of over 75, 000 peasants huddled into a single state farm whose produce he and his Communist government took away for whatever token of appreciation they deemed fit to give the peasants. This terribly demotivated the peasants. Their agricultural production drastically plummeted. China, consequently, suffered the historic famine of 1959 – 1960 where over 20 million people, almost twice the population of Zambia, perished. The Great Leap Forward turned out to be the Great Flop Backward. And with it Mao's superhuman status took a severe downsizing. The Chinese Communist Party itself stripped him of the Presidency (Head of State) of the People's Republic of China and replaced him with Liu Shaoqi (1898 – 1969), a senior leader in the Communist Party of China who professed liberal economic views and was widely held by many in the CCP, China, and the world at large as Mao's imminent successor. Mao became so unpopular following the tragedy of his Great Leap Forward that the CCP only spared his famous 'Chairmanship' (Supreme Leader) of the CCP and that of the country for fear of sparking more civil and political calamities in China.

Unlike Joseph Stalin, however, Mao Zedong was repentant. Professor Luo in his paper writes that, "With the failure of the Great Leap Forward and Communisation in 1960, Mao recognised that unless the incentive of property rights were restored to some extent, the economy as a whole could not be maintained." For some time he seemed in agreement with the President of the People's Republic of China, Liu Shaoqi, who was now earnestly spearheading policies of liberal economic reconstruction in China.

But still failing to come to terms with the prospect of granting millions and millions of his people property rights, according to Professor Luo he was still bent on *"realising the ideal of eliminating property rights"* in China, and, above all, realising that allowing liberal economic reforms to succeed in China would only entrench into people's minds the then common view that their proponent, Liu Shaoqi, was but the de facto new leader of China, Mao beat a hasty and equally disastrous retreat. He launched, in 1966, the infamous Cultural Revolution, a murderous campaign against all perceived advocates of liberal economic reforms in China. He incited Chinese youths to band up into rabid gangs, which became known as Red Guards, and physically attack, maim, humiliate, and lynch suspected Chinese liberals and, indeed, foreign liberals based in China. Mayhem engulfed China as the Red Guards ferociously attacked writers, journalists, teachers, lecturers, economists, politicians, and foreign diplomats. Schools, colleges, and universities were forced to close; temples and foreign embassies were destroyed—the British embassy was completely burnt to ashes. And Liu Shaoqi himself, the leader of liberal economic reforms in China, was officially denounced as the number one *"Capitalist-roader"* and traitor. He was subsequently expelled from the Chinese Communist Party, dismissed from government, arrested, denied medical attention for his diabetes and pneumonia ailments, and publicly beaten and humiliated by the Red Guards, and finally murdered and his remains ignominiously and secretly disposed of by state agents. And as if he was the target of the entire Cultural Revolution, his demise in 1969 brought all its mayhem to an abrupt end.

The wide repercussions of Mao Zedong's fierce opposition to liberal economic reforms in China which would have granted the people property rights as incentives for their economic prosperity were that throughout his leadership millions of Chinese peasants were trapped in perpetual poverty. Professor Luo attests that by *"1976, at the time Mao died, more than one third of China's 800 million rural population fell into the collective poverty trap.... The food shortage was so serious in some rural areas in the middle of 1970s that the local government had to issue special permits to thousands of peasants, allowing them to beg in cities."*

Therefore, the much envied economic success in China is a fairly recent phenomenon. It was literally achieved over Mao Zedong's dead body and, ironically, with the same liberal economic policies he so much abhorred. Indeed, in a strange twist of historic events, Liu Shaoqi's fellow *"Capitalist-roader,"* Deng Xiaoping (1904 – 1997) succeeded Mao Zedong. Deng Xiaoping equally suffered but 'miraculously' survived the Cultural Revolution persecution for his own liberal economic views. During the Cultural Revolution the Red Guards usually treated Deng Xiaoping as Liu Shaoqi's twin *"Capitalist-roader,"* as some of their archival Cultural Revolution posters depict. And acknowledging Liu Shaoqi as his true political and economic soul mate, his twin *"Capitalist-roader,"* Deng Xiaoping boldly reintroduced Liu's liberal economic reforms in China. Liberating the Chinese people from Communist inspired abhorrence of wealth, he memorably declared that *"To get rich is not a crime."* Walking his talk, he had the remains of Liu Shaoqi traced, retrieved, and accorded a State Funeral in 1980 and declared him a great Chinese leader who was merely unjustly treated and hounded out of power and whose ideas were viable and imperative for China's economic and political survival. Thus as though in according his departed companion a decent burial he was seeking his permission to implement his ideas to the letter, he thence forth swiftly went on to neutralise Chinese Communism with huge doses of liberal economic policies. He allowed the communes to be divided up among individual peasants, all though he fell short of granting them title deeds. According to Professor Luo, Deng Xiaoping *"restored economic freedom for most Chinese peasants, and legitimised private rights over most assets except full private ownership of farmland."* Nevertheless, it's thanks to that much liberal economic reform that China's economic fortunes tremendously improved to the envy of many countries in the world. But above all, this entire Chinese economic and political 'Long March' from the feudalistic Qing dynasty to Deng Xiaoping's epoch-making liberal reforms has proved beyond everything else what an incentive property ownership, especially land ownership, is in an economy.

Taking into consideration how China's economic and political landscape has virtually been shaped by its people's historic endeavours to own their lands and property, its tragic negation of those endeavours, and the phenomenal economic success it has eventually recorded by merely conceding, albeit partially, those endeavours to its people, Professor Luo could not help conclude his paper with an unmistakable hint of unwavering admonition: *"China, in this tortuous process, paid a terrible price and accumulated a lot of lesson and wisdom. Its current land system is far from perfect, and is in need of fundamental reform."*

Thus, if any Bantu African government genuinely wants to learn from China, to prosper like China, they have to be wary of "the terrible price" China paid for denying its people their land and property ownership aspirations and rights; and they have to learn "a lot of lesson and wisdom" it has "tortuously accumulated" over its land management or mismanagement. How it imparts positively or negatively on a country's and, indeed, individual citizen's economies, and be warned that China itself is not resting on its laurels as it is still "in need of fundamental land reform" with the ultimate goal of granting its people "full private ownership of farmland."

8

La

Luta

Continua

The truth is that we are not yet free; we have merely achieved the freedom to be free, the right not to be oppressed. We have not taken the final step of our journey, but the first step on a longer and even more difficult road....

I have walked that long road to freedom. I have tried not to

*falter; I have made missteps along the way. But I have discovered
the secret that after climbing a great hill, one only finds that there
are many more hills to climb. I have taken a moment here to rest,
to steal a view of the glorious vista that surrounds me, to look back
on the distance I have come. But I can rest only for a moment ...
and I dare not linger, for my long walk is not yet ended.*

—Nelson Mandela

*Our common African culture allows me to say to those of you who
are younger that we charge you with the responsibility of leading
our people and continent into the new world of the next century
[21st century] which must be an African century.*

—Nelson Mandela

*Our young people of this generation, appear less committed and
less passionate in terms of embracing the values which propelled
all of us to fight for independence and also to fight for the
economic emancipation of our people ... I would like to see a little
more commitment on the part of the younger generation to
embrace the ideas and ideals for which we fought.*

—Vernon Johnson Mwaanga (VJ)

Indeed in the 1960s our forefathers ejected colonialists from our
governments and reclaimed our autonomy; and in the 1990s our
mothers and fathers ejected totalitarian Bantu African rulers and
reclaimed our liberty; and now in the 2010s we, the sons and
daughters of Bantu Africa, *"those of [us] who are younger,"* the
"young people of this generation," as Nelson Mandela and Vernon
Mwaanga (b. 1943), a prominent Zambian liberationist,
respectively put it, are *"charged with the responsibility of leading
our people"* in ejecting Bantu African oligarchies and reclaim our

lands and property, our inheritance, our birth right, and complete the attainment of all three fundamental Bantu African liberation causes our ancestors embarked on almost a millennium ago, the realisation of *"the ideas and ideals for which [they] fought."*

In essence our millennium-long liberation movement closely resembles the advancement of a spacecraft into space whereby at every pivotal stage disused rockets are ejected from its mechanism. And now in Bantu Africa time is up for our oligarchies. They have nothing more to offer; and they have even openly testified to that effect, that they are now in government only "to eat," to enrich themselves, their families and friends by looting our natational treasures through obscene self-salary increments, allowances, and gratuities, remember Daniel Munkombwe's testimony that we saw in chapter 6. But more crucially Bantu African oligarchies are now the bane of our cause to reclaim our lands and property just as colonialists and totalitarian rulers were respectively the bane of our autonomy and liberty. For lack of political will they simply will not allow us in our millions to *"freely"* reclaim our lands and property. Again like colonialists who claimed that we, Bantu Africans, had enough room in which to exercise our autonomy in Bantu Africa in reference to Bantu African reserves and homelands they crammed our forefathers into under their colonial administration, and totalitarian Bantu African rulers who would contend that their governments were nothing but *"participatory democracies"* which upheld all our liberties, they, Bantu African oligarchies, would want us believe that we already have sufficient laws that grant us *"equitable access to land and associated resources; and security of land rights for land holders,"* as stated in article 293 of Zambia's proposed new constitution which now President Sata doesn't want to be enacted any time soon. Indeed, in itself an example of Bantu African governments' lack of political will to realise their people's aspirations, President Sata, on 30th November, 2013, after seeing his government spend billions of

Kwacha and three years in which it made the entire Zambian society—professors, cabinet ministers, members of parliament, judges, lawyers, church leaders, bankers, businessmen, non-governmental organisations, traditional rulers, councillors, teachers, health practitioners, soldiers, policemen, students, the disabled, pupils, and peasants—dedicate their time, efforts, expertise, and experiences to coming up with a draft of this new constitution containing many such progressive laws which will empower the currently underprivileged vast majority of Zambians, stunned Zambians with a casual but typical Bantu African oligarchy remark saying Zambia did not, after all, need a constitution but amendments to defective laws in its current constitution. And he followed this with a formal instruction to his ministers and permanent secretaries to simply ignore widespread calls for the enactment of this new constitution.

The truth is that Bantu African masses cannot afford to own their lands and property by any laws passed by Bantu African oligarchies. Bantu African oligarchies still do not want the majority of their people to own their lands and property. They systematically place their laws above the reach of their masses, and that is why they prefer passing laws by mere amendments in parliaments which they control rather than through referenda where the masses have a direct say. Only Bantu African oligarchies themselves, their few rich friends, and wealthy foreigners can and do regularly utilise their laws by flexing their huge financial muscles.

The noble aspiration of "equitable access to land and associated resources; and security of land rights for land holders;" will only become a reality if we, Bantu Africans are all "equitably" allowed to "FREELY" own, develop, and secure our lands and property, just as we were allowed to *"FREELY"* govern ourselves in the 1960s and to "FREELY" elect our leaders in the 1990s.

Bantu African lands and associated resources are our entitlement, our inheritance, our birth right, and they should be granted to us all FREELY as any of our rights. No one buys his own birth right, entitlement or inheritance unless something scandalous is afoot, unless somebody wicked wants to cheat him out of his own inheritance. And most Bantu African oligarchies, their few rich friends, and wealthy foreigners, from South Africa to South Sudan, who now expect ordinary Bantu Africans to spend a fortune to secure their own lands and property did themselves acquire and secure their vast lands and properties with a bottle of wine, a pack of cigarettes, and a fire-arm presented to some gullible Bantu African chief as 'priceless gifts.' And for a bottle of wine, a pack of cigarettes, and an odd firearm, some of them acquired and secured vast swaths of Bantu Africa's richest land on outrageous 999 leases.

In any case, while Bantu Africa's rich acquired and secured their vast lands and properties for a song largely to indulge their avarice, ordinary Bantu Africans need the ownership and security of their small pieces of lands and small properties for survival. We, poor Bantu Africans, need the ownership and security of our lands and property to emancipate ourselves from the shackles of poverty, to overcome our perpetual want and deprivation. We need the ownership and security of our small pieces of lands and small properties to raise capital and embark on countrywide manufacturing and processing industries that will give us fulfilling and better paying jobs that will effectively combat our mass unemployment and abject poverty.

This momentous undertaking of overcoming our mass unemployment and abject poverty which Nelson Mandela recognises to be *"even more difficult,"* than those we have so far accomplished, autonomy and liberty, is beyond the grasp of Bantu African oligarchies. And they have long demonstrated this as well.

In an obvious attempt to sound relevant and equal to the task of overcoming our mass unemployment and abject poverty, they, however, vociferously claim to equally want to provide jobs and create wealth for the majority of Bantu Africans. But practically they still let our cotton, copper, coffee, cocoa, and so forth exported raw to Asia, Europe, and the Americas and almost all our needs: clothes, beddings, needles, toiletries, and so forth imported from there, just like in colonial times. Now, any leader who genuinely seeks to provide jobs and create wealth for his people cannot let that happen because jobs and wealth lie between bales of cotton and bales of jeans trousers, between raw materials and manufactured products. By letting their countries export raw materials, Bantu African oligarchies are equally exporting the jobs of processing and manufacturing them into daily needs they entail. And by importing these daily needs we are actually paying foreign workers in Bangladesh, China, Korea, Italy, Japan, and so forth for turning our cotton, leather, copper, etc., into jeans trousers, blankets, shoes, radios, and mobile phones. Well-paying processing and manufacturing jobs we can easily retain and do by simply holding onto our raw materials and raising the necessary capital from our lands and properties, if only Bantu African governments would let us own and secure them.

Again, prompted by expediency more than anything else, wily Bantu African oligarchies also occasionally do acknowledge the economic need to grant land and property ownership to Bantu Africans. But aware that they have no more political will to right away lead us into such a radical programme which will cement our emancipation, they deliberately dawdle and stall over obsolete and irrelevant considerations and procedures. Zambia's President Michael Sata, again, announced upon coming to power in 2011 that he would consult with Zambian chiefs about granting Zambians land tenure. Two years later on 15 May 2013, he announced, through his press aide, that *"In order to encourage progressive farmers to make long term investment in customary land, our government in consultation with chiefs and other traditional authorities will introduce legislation to ensure security of tenure for such land."* And 4 years before Sata became President in Zambia, the strong man of Uganda, President Yoweri Museveni (b. 1944), took a similar path to land ownership reforms in his country only to stall over the Baganda King, the Kabaka, who incidentally is also traditionally known as the *"Sabataka,"* which means the owner of all land. In a BBC Focus on Africa magazine of July-September 2009 Joshua M'mali in an article entitled '*A Kingdom for a Vote,*' reported that:

After meeting with the Prime Minister [of Buganda Kingdom], known as the Katikiro of Buganda, Museveni recently agreed to shelve proposed amendments to the 1998 Land Reform Act. These would have modernised and democratised land ownership in the country, thus disempowering the Kabaka and his family of a claim to vast swathes of land.

But since Bantu Africans reclaimed self-rule and became republics, with the exception of Swaziland and Lesotho, Bantu African chiefs and kings have been political misfits who have no real business in Bantu Africans' political and economic affairs. They have no bearing whatsoever in any Bantu African government's policy making. And Zambia's President Sata himself has amply demonstrated this since coming to power. He has declared every remote township in Zambia into a district, instantly removing them and the huge chunks of lands surrounding them from the control of chiefs and placing them in the hands of local government councils, without the knowledge or approval of chiefs. If not for procrastination as a result of lack of political will, why should he now turn to them for consultations over granting land ownership to individual Bantu Africans?

In any case, for Bantu African governments to consult with Bantu African chiefs in their land reforms is like a school teacher consulting with his school bullies if he should let his pupils freely stroll around the school premises. In both the current and proposed new constitutions of Zambia the main *"concept and principles relating to the institution of chiefs [is to] hold assets or properties in trust for itself and the people under a chiefs jurisdiction."* The assets and properties in question are vast swaths of so-called customary lands or native lands and houses, huts, shops, granaries, kraals, fields, farms, and gardens therein of over 80% of Bantu Africans who live *"under a chief's jurisdiction."* This whole arrangement is diabolic, exploitative, and retrogressive. It leaves over 80% of Bantu Africans open to our proverbial systematic dispossession. No one, except an exploitative estate administrator, holds in trust assets and properties of a mature and grown up man. Bantu Africans came of age the moment they reclaimed their self-determination in the 1960s. That is when they should have been granted their inheritance, their secured own lands and properties. Individual Bantu Africans or households should each have equally reclaimed, owned and begun to independently administer their lands and property like any mature citizens do in the free republics of Europe, America, and Asia. The universal principle of self-determination followed to its logical conclusion does not end at national level, as is the case in most of Bantu Africa, but flows down to local authorities as decentralisation and all the way down to families and individuals as privatisation or private ownership.

And nothing has so much exposed glaring failures by Bantu African governments to successfully govern their countries and people than awkwardly entrusting their people's lands and properties to Bantu African chiefs. In entrusting over 80% of such lands and properties to Bantu African chiefs, they have ceded responsibility of over 80% of their countries, so much so that their governments are little more than municipal authorities in essence and structure. Latin America may have its banana republics but Bantu Africa surely has municipal republics, very much similar to ancient Greece's city-states, as they only practically exist and operate in Bantu African urban places. They rarely make their presence or governance felt in the lands they have entrusted to chiefs (80%of all Bantu Africa) that, indeed, Bantu Africa is not only underdeveloped but under-governed. The chiefs to whom they entrust their people's welfare are never funded or supported with resources or qualified staff to administer their people's vast estates under them. And to make matters worse most of these Bantu African chiefs are themselves ill-educated that they don't even understand that they only hold in trust their people's assets and properties. Like the Sabataka, *the owner of all land in Uganda*," they regard everything in their chiefdoms as their God-given largesse to squander at will. Probably to redress their own want or out of sheer wastefulness they give away huge swathes of lands and vast acres of forests to foreign investors in exchange of second-hand cars, small amounts of money and a few herds of livestock far below the value of these resources of their people. And sometimes overwhelmed by the sheer volume of resources at their disposal they do not even care how and who is depleting them absolutely for free. The day I typed this, March 4, 2014, Zambia's ZNBC TV reported and showed a scam where truckloads of red wood (mukula trees) were leaving Chief Nyalugwe's area (in the Eastern Province of Zambia) for a lucrative market in China without his knowledge and under fake authorisation purported to be from Zambia's Forestry Department. It's as if the trees being felled rampantly by all sorts of people either for this illegal logging or charcoal burning and the lands thus deforested belong to no one in particular and as such everyone is free to exploit them at will. Consequently, a customary or native land in Bantu Africa is an open wound, bleeding, oozing pus, and repeatedly getting gashed, lacerated, and infected with no one trying to dress it.

Yet even this now gangrenous problem of neglect and waste in 80% of Bantu Africa would vanish like a bout of acne in adolescence by simply letting individual Bantu Africans themselves to own their lands, resources, and properties. If we, individual Bantu Africans, could own our lands, resources, and properties therein, we would guard them jealously and would never allow any body to abuse them. A Bantu Africa of titled individual land and property owners is a secured Bantu Africa. And, accordingly, Bantu African chiefs with their perverse role of guardians of our *"assets and properties"* will finally get their marching orders. They would practically become redundant. And they themselves *know this too well. In reaction to a proposed* article in Zambia's new constitution which seeks to vest all land in the President, one Zambian chief, Chief Puta, categorically told the Zambian Daily Mail Newspaper of June 15, 2013 that:

We have a problem with the draft constitution on the issue of land. We are chiefs because of land. It is not safe for all the land to be vested in the President. A bad President could in future sell customary land in a chiefdom and leave a chief with nothing.

And a good President? Certainly he is not one who let chiefs possess customary lands and deprive ordinary Bantu Africans of land and property ownership, emasculating them of their economic ability, but one who must now and in future distribute for FREE, in fact RETURN is the word, one who must now and in future RETURN customary lands in chiefdoms to individual Bantu Africans, one who must now and in future enable individual Bantu

Africans thrive economically and relieve chiefs of their uncalled-for role of being guardians, selfish guardians for that matter, of Bantu Africans 'lands and properties.

There is nothing beneficial to ordinary Bantu Africans about Bantu African chieftaincy that they would miss if it ends up abolished or chiefs rendered redundant. Chief Puta and any Bantu African chief who shares his sentiments are solely crying for their own privileges and interests and those of their sons and nephews and not for those of ordinary Bantu Africans under their jurisdiction. Since time immemorial chiefs and their institutions have instead been a scourge of ordinary Bantu Africans under their jurisdiction. European slavers enlisted them to capture their own people into slavery. Colonial governments engaged them to compel their people to pay poll tax or surrender them up for servitude, "Chibalo". Totalitarian Bantu African governments and Bantu African oligarchies now use them to extort loyalty and compliance from their people with threats of eviction from their chiefdoms. Therefore, a good 21st century President must not hesitate to promptly bring to an end their treacherous institution which has menaced Bantu Africans for a thousand years now.

If it is for the unmistakable role of the only discernible authority in 80% of Bantu Africa which is under-governed, a good President and his 21st century Bantu African government, in pursuit of effective governance, must see to it that capable elected officials take charge of chiefdoms and govern them as, say, counties with fully fledged county officials and employees who apart from effecting the development of their counties and providing amenities to county dwellers they will facilitate or undertake to grant land and property ownership to them.

But such transformation, such radical changes in the governance of Bantu Africa, such pro-ordinary Bantu Africans restructuring of Bantu African governance, can only be brought about by nothing short of a mass-driven full scale REVOLUTION. Cosmetic changes or amendments, as President Sata advocates, to current Bantu African constitutions whose adoption and enactment largely rests with parliaments and Presidents compromised by Bantu African oligarchies can never fully yield that transformed Bantu Africa. Just as no colonial parliament ever granted self-determination to any Bantu African people; and no Bantu African totalitarian parliament ever granted liberty to their people. It had to take Bantu African masses themselves to not only overthrow colonialism and totalitarianism but also their respective compromised parliaments and replace them with new ones that championed their causes.

Thus there can be no shirking Nelson Mandela's charge that those of us who are younger, those of us who were born in the freedom and liberty that our forefathers, fathers, and mothers reclaimed, we, the Bantu African masses of today, have the responsibility to overthrow the impoverishing status-quo and further emancipate ourselves economically, "the responsibility of leading our people and continent into the new world of the 21st century which must be an African century."

Emancipating a people from oppression, exploitation, and impoverishment is always a bottom to top operation; never top to bottom. No oppressor or exploiter has ever come down from his mansions to lead the oppressed, exploited, and impoverished into his mansions. The best he can do, if he is benevolent, is to let them shelter in his barns, like giving colonial subjects certain freedoms, homelands, native reserves, but never autonomy over their countries; the best Bantu African oligarchies can do is to allow the Bantu African masses to merely cultivate their pieces of lands but never to own them. So like in the struggles against colonialism and totalitarianism the Bantu African masses have no viable option but to overthrow Bantu African oligarchies and their impoverishing systems if they are to get themselves titled lands and properties which will help them secure capital and industrialise their production. Just as our forefathers, fathers and mothers respectively voted for Bantu African autonomy and liberty by voting into government devoted champions of these causes, today's ordinary Bantu African masses have to literally vote for their own titled lands, farms, gardens, houses, and shops and access to capital by voting into power people they genuinely believe will grant them land and property ownership.

As far back as the 1990s Zambia's former President, the late Frederick Chiluba who himself successfully led a mass revolution that ousted Kenneth Kaunda's totalitarian regime, anticipated the vast majority of impoverished and neglected ordinary Bantu Africans whom he simply described as the "rural poor," those who dwell in 80% of under-governed Bantu Africa under the jurisdiction of chiefs, to once more revolt against Bantu African oligarchies and their impoverishing systems. But he played down their success citing lack of resources and logistics with which to overthrow Bantu African oligarchies and their solidly established systems. He wrote in his book, *Democracy, the Challenge of Change:*

The largest single social and occupational group in Zambia still comprises the peasantry and the great majority of Zambia's poor have always been rural poor. A failure by the government to redress the traditional imbalance which has favoured urban dwellers could compel the peasantry to switch their support away from [the governing party]. A peasant party as such would probably be financially and organisationally weak. Support from the large and medium-scale farmers could not be relied upon. They are not poor and they already enjoy a significant channel for approaching the government, through their National Farmers

Union.

But, President Chiluba must have forgotten that Bantu Africans all over Bantu Africa did not have lots of money and logistics to overthrow rich and well established colonial governments. And, true, many Bantu Africans who were themselves already rich and comfortable under colonial administrations tended to side with colonial governments and were reluctant to fully support independence struggles. But in spite of that poor Bantu Africans in Southern Sudan, Uganda, Kenya, Tanzania, D.R. Congo, Zambia, Malawi, Zimbabwe, Angola, Botswana, Namibia, Mozambique, South Africa and so forth emerged victorious and formed governments that advanced their cause of self-determination.

Be might and brutal the force that stands in the way of an afflicted people in revolt, an afflicted people in revolt will always overcome it. Not because of whatever resources and organisational abilities such a people may have but because it always draws overwhelming power from its very affliction, an enormous power generated by its torment, pain, anguish, want, humiliation and despair which the rich and might can never have or contend with because they do not understand it. Yes, those not afflicted, be them rich that they can buy the entire Bantu Africa with their fortune and militarily mighty that they can conquer the entire world at the touch of a single key on a computer, never know and feel the strength of this power until it sweeps them away from their palaces. And so it was that from the affliction of one impoverished 26-year-old Tunisian street vendor, Mohammed Bouazizi (1984 – 2011), who out of it set himself ablaze on 17 December, 2010, sprung the overwhelming Arab Spring Revolution that toppled and trounced the formidable governments and mighty forces of President Zine el Abidine Ben Ali (b. 1936) in Tunisia itself,

President Hosni Mubarak (b. 1928) in Egypt, and President Colonel Muammar Gaddafi (1942 – 2011) in Libya. And long before Bouaziz could trigger the Arab Spring from his affliction which, in essence, was merely an epitome of the affliction of the vast majorities of ordinary Arab masses in North Africa, the legendary US Senator and Attorney General, Robert F. Kennedy (1925 – 1968), an ardent civil rights champion himself, drew abiding lessons from many instances throughout the world where the oppressed, the afflicted, have risen against all odds to overcome their mighty oppressors and redress their affliction. He noted: *"Each time a man stands up for an ideal, or acts to improve the lot of others, or strikes out against injustice, he sends forth a tiny ripple of hope, and crossing each other from a million different centres of energy and daring, those ripples build a current that can sweep down the mightiest walls of oppression and resistance."*

So never mind the poor Bantu African masses' lack of resources and logistics to accomplish a successful revolt. As long as they are tormented by widespread deprivation and poverty so long and widespread will be their revolt and redress. Their torment, pain, anguish, want, humiliation and despair and the astounding power they pack is the eye of their looming revolution and not anyone's money and logistics. It is that phenomenal power which will whip up ferocious winds of change that, like a hurricane, will rout Bantu African oligarchies and their impoverishing systems across the length and breadth of Bantu Africa so much so that Bantu Africa will emerge totally transformed.

The effect alone of ordinary Bantu African masses finally owning their lands and properties and thereby be enabled to access capital to industrialise their production will in its wake burst our colonial drawn boundaries at the seams. Bantu African state boundaries will not withstand the pressure that will ensue from their industrialisation. Bantu African industrial products will seek an immediate vast viable domestic market such as the entire Bantu Africa itself with its population of over half a billion people. This will erode our state boundaries and render them unnecessary and unmanageable. Eventually necessary economic but also political and social re-organisation of the entire Bantu Africa will kick in.

Bantu Africa will coalesce into one indivisible political, social, and economic entity; and the vestiges of colonial drawn frontiers, frontier workers, their resources, and activities, will be driven to the real fringes of Bantu Africa to man its gateways to the outside world and keep at bay foreign industrial products that would adversely compete with Bantu Africa's. With its own industrialisation running at full throttle Bantu Africa will definitely cease to be an open market for every foreign industrial product, it will cease to provide mass employment and fat salaries for foreign workers and preserve them for her own people. No industrialised market, no matter how liberal, is an open market to every foreign industrial product. Only at the dawn of the 21st century, October 2000, did the USA deliberately pass the African Growth and Opportunity Act (AGOA) to grant US market access for selected Bantu African countries' industrial products. Otherwise Bantu Africa's products like other foreign industrial products from Europe, Asia, and elsewhere were barred from entering the USA by deliberately placed high tariffs, outright bans, and other measures such as subsidising local production. Similarly, in an industrialised one Bantu Africa high tariffs will certainly have to be imposed on all foreign industrial products to protect, nurture and sustain its industrial efforts and production. And the revenues thus raised could be used to generate more hydro electricity from Bantu Africa's mostly untapped hydro-power potential and make electricity readily available for more and further Bantu African industrial activities.

Of course, for Bantu African oligarchies all this, an industrialised and politically, socially, and economically integrated Bantu Africa which can stand up to China, India, Europe, America, and all for its own good, is a far-fetched dream, a near impossibility. In his book, *A Humanist in Africa*, Zambia's Kenneth Kaunda dismissed it as a mere *"emotional identification of the people with their brothers over the horizon."* And his successor and protégé, President Michael Sata, in May 2013 at the 50th African Union heads of states summit in Addis Ababa, Ethiopia, utterly rejected a proposal for Bantu Africans to at least consider carrying one common passport in the near future. He said, *"Zambia makes its own laws. So, no to one African passport."* And one blogger who described himself as an *"economics advisor at the Zambian Embassy in Addis Ababa,"* hailed Sata saying, *"It was a courageous move on a continent where people cannot face up to reality, and I give full marks to him. The African Union spends a lot of time and of course money debating ideas which are not practical or whose time simply hasn't come."* Incidentally Bantu African leaders for the idea of *"one African passport"* only adopted it as part of their **Vision 2063**, implying that even them only envisage it to be actualised 50 years from now.

Understandably, at the moment when the majority of Bantu Africans do not own their lands and property, political, social, and economic integration is a scary proposition, one many Bantu Africans would comfortably see deferred indefinitely. It evokes fears of further surrendering their lands, resources, and properties to a common Bantu African trust even before they have made sure that they are really theirs, that they are indeed their stakes which will bring them corresponding dividends at the end of the day. They have not yet secured their lands and property; they fear to pool them together with those of their brothers and sisters knowing it will be difficult to relocate them and the dividends they will accrue to their names. But once all have secured their lands and property, pooling them for a common goal will become easy and logical. Easy because they will all know what will be due to each of them based on their respective stakes; and logical because they will now all seek to maximise their returns on their respective stakes through stronger joint operations. Thus have companies and multinationals been formed throughout the world.

Clearly land and property ownership for all Bantu Africans is the master key to Bantu Africa's development, to the illusive political, social, and economic transformation of Bantu Africa, to the much sought after prosperity of Bantu Africa and Bantu Africans, to the long heralded African renaissance.

So once more, and in the prompting words of Nelson Mandela and Robert Kennedy, the onus is on those of us "*who are younger*", those of us who are yet to make our contribution to the emancipation of Bantu Africa, "*to stand up for the ideal*", for the noble cause of land and property ownership by all our people, to act to "*improve the lot of*" our people, to "*strike out against injustice*", against the systematic disposition and impoverishment of our people, and "*send forth tiny ripples of hope that will cross each other from a million different centres of energy and daring and build a current that will sweep down the mightiest walls of suppression and resistance*" erected by Bantu African oligarchies. And the sagacious Thabo Mbeki warns:

Africa cannot renew herself where its upper echelons are a mere parasite on the rest of society, enjoying a self-endowed mandate to use their political power and define the uses of such power such that its exercise ensures that our continent reproduces itself as the periphery of the world economy. Poor, underdeveloped, and incapable of development.

The African renaissance demands that we purge ourselves of the parasites….

And as Nelson Mandela again says, we *"dare not linger,"* we cannot afford to wait for the actualisation of vision 2063: an entire generation of 4 000 million Bantu Africans who now live in abject poverty will perish in misery and never come to know good decent lives. And with this menacing spectre persistently haunting Bantu Africa, Thabo Mbeki declares that: *"The time has come that we say enough and no more, and by acting to banish the shame remake ourselves as the midwives of the African renaissance."*

And then Vincent Bakpetu in his book, *Africa and Unity*, has enduring words of exhortation for those of us who are younger and learned but have an inclination to procrastinate and shirk our responsibilities, those of us who, again in the words of Vernon Mwaanga, who was himself a young liberationist of about 25 years old, *"appear less committed and less passionate in terms of embracing the values which propelled all of us to fight for independence and also to fight for the economic emancipation of our people…."* Bakpetu wrote in 1969 but his words, as demonstrated by Mwaanga who said the above only in 2013, are still true today:

The failure is even more deplorable on the part of you African intellectuals, especially those [of you] who have lived abroad and who should know. Rather than being the originators of good and useful ideas, [you] have sought refuge in false, self-deceptive and self-defeating desire to be objective; whatever that means. In this failing [you] show utter ignorance of European and world history. If we take the case of Europe in the nineteenth century alone, students and intellectuals were always in the vanguard, if not always in the forefront of liberal movements advocating meaningful change. In Austria and Germany, for instance, it was universities which focussed the intellectual unrest and discontent with the existing state of things, in spite of the popular feeling of economic distress. Neither factor on its own could have produced change. Both had to combine; for popular discontent in itself could not bring about desired change in the same way that ideas by themselves could not accomplish the revolution. The intellectual stimulus is always needed to shake people out of their complacency and servile conformity. This point seems not to have been grasped by [you] the scholars of Africa.... What do [you] intend to make to [your nation] in order to achieve more than stagnation? These questions are crucial; for, without them, [the quest of emancipating Bantu Africans from poverty] will never go beyond the confines of Conference Halls and costly banquets.

So stand up, brother; lead the way and liberate our people from soulless toil. Rise, sister, suckle us knowledge and courage that we may not falter and procrastinate in answering this solemn calling to serve our nation. Come, brother, laluta continua, be our new Jomo Kenyatta and Nelson Mandela. But this time emancipate our people from systematic dispossession, peasantry, and poverty. Let them reclaim their lands and properties so that they are able to process their food and produce and manufacture their own goods. Hurry, sister, laluta continua, be our new Queen Nzinga; but this time unite us around a fire of industrialisation that will burn down our colonial drawn boundaries and forge us one indivisible prosperous Bantu Africa.

George Malonje Mwanza is a passionate researcher, non-fiction writer, small-scale livestock farmer and businessman, and chess player.

He was born in Zambia in 1971. His father was a military instructor at Zambia Military Academy (ZMA). Upon his father's resignation from the army, he and his family went to live a rural life as peasant farmers at Sinda, Eastern Zambia. It is from there he went to Tiritonse Primary School and Katete Secondary School.

Upon his completion of secondary school, he was selected to pursue university education at the University of Zambia in 1991. Instead, he chose to go and study for the Catholic priesthood at Emmaus Spirituality Centre in Lusaka and Mpima Major Seminary in Kabwe. In 1994 he obtained a diploma in philosophy and religious studies and left the Seminary.

He lived in Lusaka for 3 years with his relatives and there started researching and writing his first manuscript on African political, social, and economic affairs. Multimedia Zambia Publications accepted to publish it but they soon got liquidated before they could.

He then returned to Sinda to venture into small-scale livestock farming and businesses.

In 2007 the government of Zambia in collaboration with the Chinese government sponsored him to attend a month-long seminar at Zhejiang University in China on 'Small-scale Farmers Adapting to Global Markets. Upon his return from China he embarked on researching and putting together this book.

He now lives in Sinda married with 5 children and on a piece of land which his chief categorically told him to never attempt to get title deeds for it as it was a customary land.

www.ingramcontent.com/pod-product-compliance
Lightning Source LLC
Chambersburg PA
CBHW060247290526
45789CB00001B/231

9781501068546